W9-BXX-575

THE GREAT ESCAPE

How a few Somali girls changed the world after escaping from the bondage of female circumcision.

A short story

Yasin
I hope this story will
Inspire you and you
can involve this issue

Farah M. Mohamed
Washington DC
6/13/2015

I

Copyright @ 2014
Farah M. Mohamed

All rights reserved, no part of this book may be produced,
scanned, or distributed in any printed or electronic form
without permission. Please do not participate in or
encourage piracy of copyrighted materials in violation of the
author's rights. Purchase only authorized editions.

Published by Somali Media Company
4900 Leesburg Pike, Suite 413
Alexandria, VA 22302
www.somalimedia.com
publish@somalimedia.com

The Library of Congress Control Number: 2013923715
Mohamed, Farah M
The Great Escape: *How a few Somali girls changed the world,*
after escaping from the bondage of female circumcision.
Graphic novel

 ISBN 978-0-9726615-6-0

First edition November 2014

Printed in the United States of America.

Other Books

- Xasuus Qor (Timelines of Somali History)
- The Miracle Boy and the Somali gangs
- Wiilkii Mucjisada ahaa iyo Budhcaddii Soomaalida
- The Somali Queen: Queen Araweelo
- Saxarla: A Somali novel

ACKNOWLEDGMENTS

I would like to thank all the Somali cultural scholars, advisors, and friends who have helped in the realization of this book. I must express gratitude to Mohamed Jama Omar (Dogox), Bashir Sheikh Omar Goth, Farhia M. Absie, Weris Jama, Hafsa A. Jama, Idil Abdi Osman, Amran Hussein Hassan, Ubah Hussein Hassan and Sindiya Darman. Thank you for all of the great advice, reviews, editing and the encouragement.

Finally, a special acknowledgement to my illustrator **Sergio Drumond** who has crafted such beautiful images.

DEDICATION

For **all** Somali **brave girls.**

ABOUT THE AUTHOR

Farah Mohamed is a short story author, novelist, and poet, both in English and his native (Somali) languages. For more than ten years, Farah worked with refugees and immigrant communities in the United States; particularly Somalis and other minorities in the Washington metropolitan area. Even though he had shown keen interest in reading and writing, since his childhood he has been deeply inspired by the refugee stories and the continued social strife of his native land.

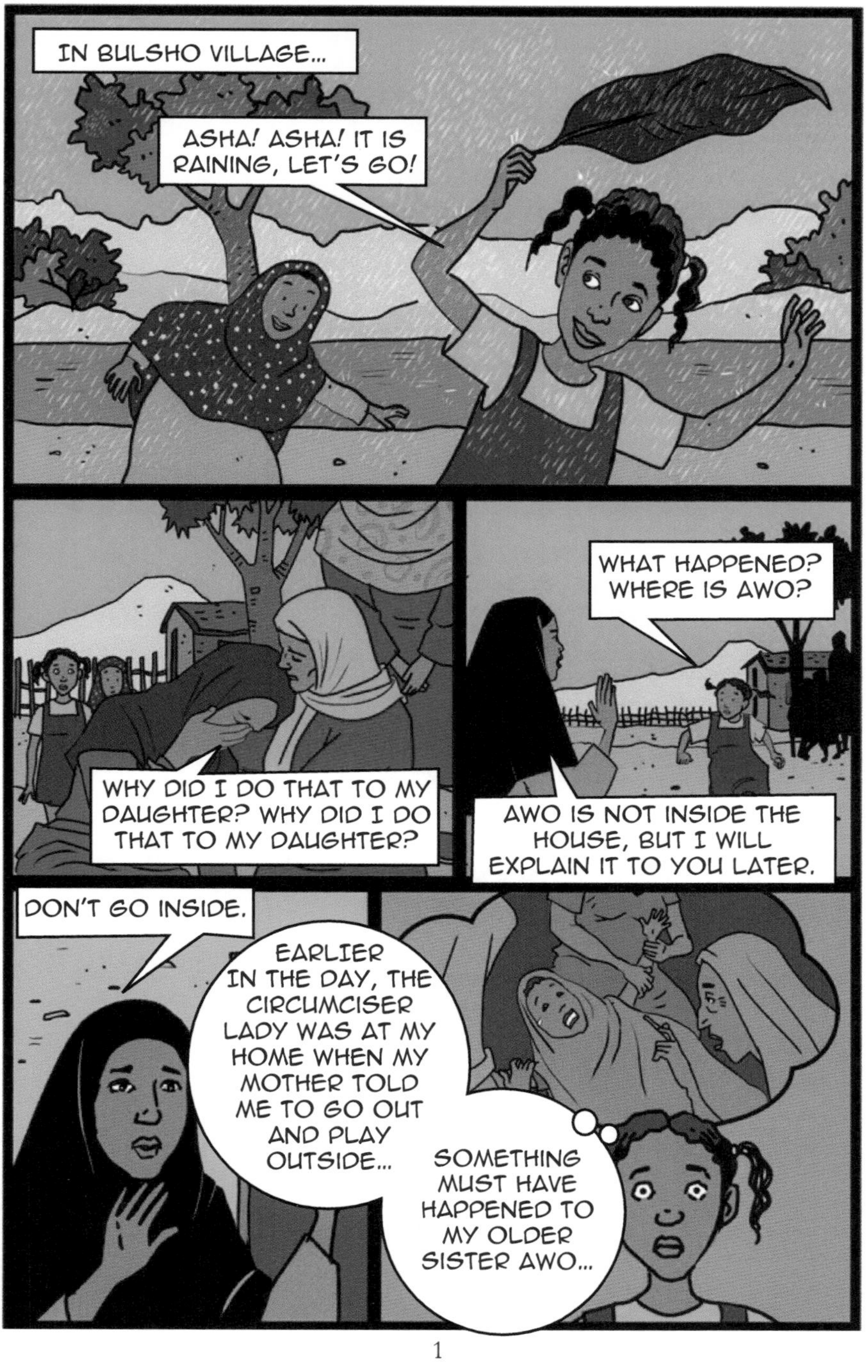
IN BULSHO VILLAGE...
ASHA! ASHA! IT IS RAINING, LET'S GO!
WHY DID I DO THAT TO MY DAUGHTER? WHY DID I DO THAT TO MY DAUGHTER?
WHAT HAPPENED? WHERE IS AWO?
AWO IS NOT INSIDE THE HOUSE, BUT I WILL EXPLAIN IT TO YOU LATER.
DON'T GO INSIDE.
EARLIER IN THE DAY, THE CIRCUMCISER LADY WAS AT MY HOME WHEN MY MOTHER TOLD ME TO GO OUT AND PLAY OUTSIDE...
SOMETHING MUST HAVE HAPPENED TO MY OLDER SISTER AWO...

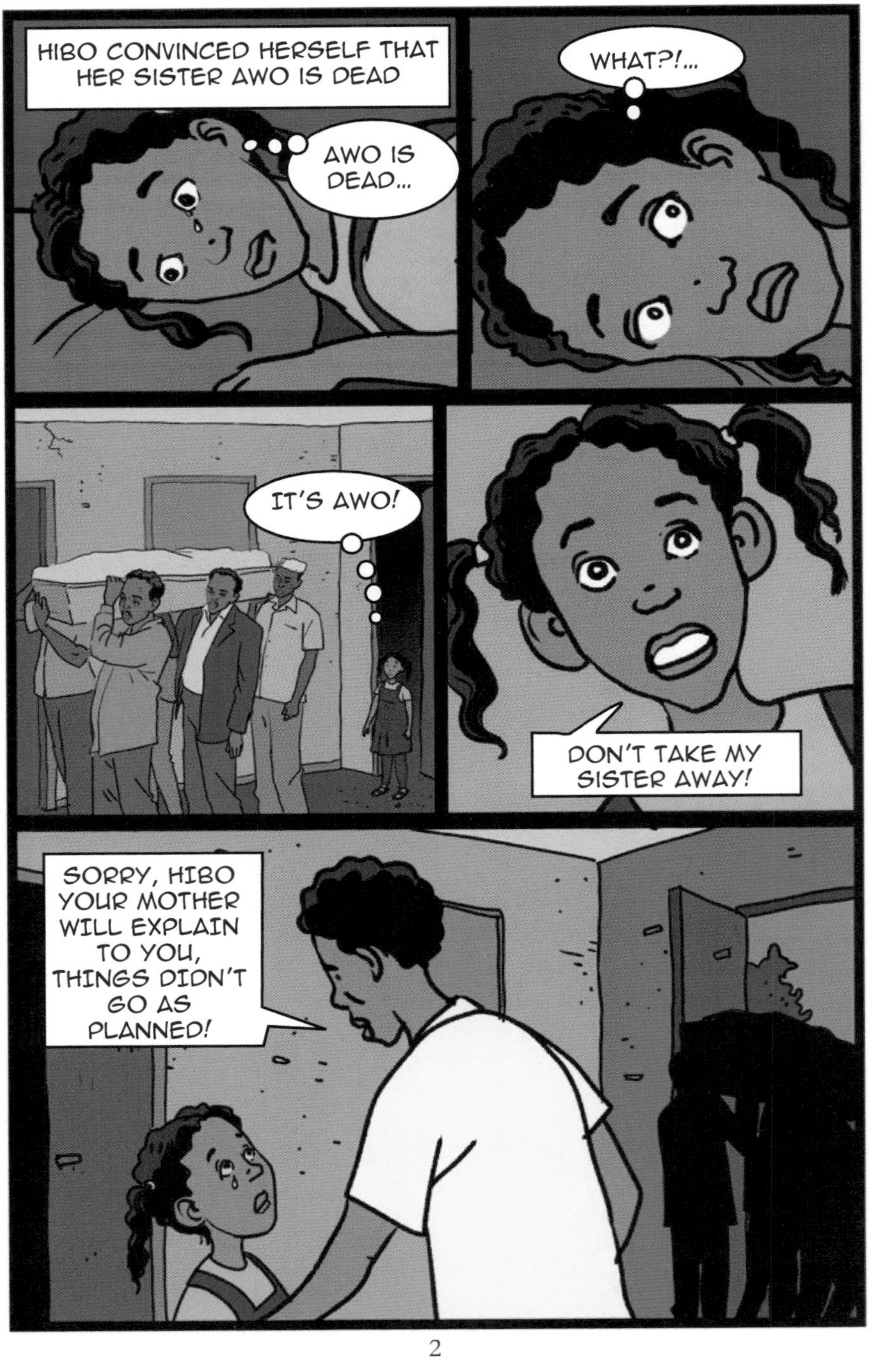
HIBO CONVINCED HERSELF THAT HER SISTER AWO IS DEAD
AWO IS DEAD...
WHAT?!...
IT'S AWO!
DON'T TAKE MY SISTER AWAY!
SORRY, HIBO YOUR MOTHER WILL EXPLAIN TO YOU, THINGS DIDN'T GO AS PLANNED!

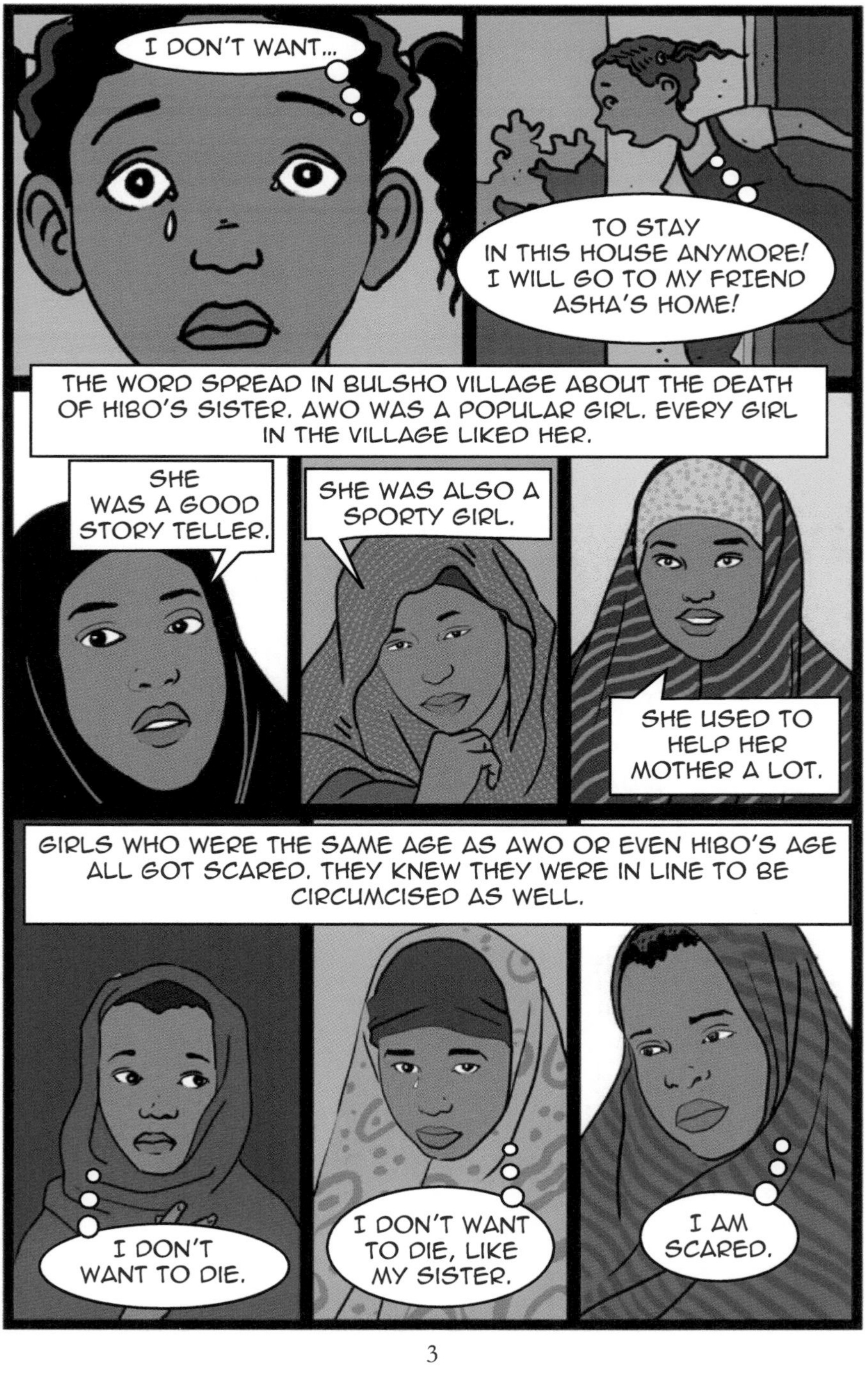
I DON'T WANT...
TO STAY IN THIS HOUSE ANYMORE! I WILL GO TO MY FRIEND ASHA'S HOME!
THE WORD SPREAD IN BULSHO VILLAGE ABOUT THE DEATH OF HIBO'S SISTER. AWO WAS A POPULAR GIRL. EVERY GIRL IN THE VILLAGE LIKED HER.
SHE WAS A GOOD STORY TELLER.
SHE WAS ALSO A SPORTY GIRL.
SHE USED TO HELP HER MOTHER A LOT.
GIRLS WHO WERE THE SAME AGE AS AWO OR EVEN HIBO'S AGE ALL GOT SCARED. THEY KNEW THEY WERE IN LINE TO BE CIRCUMCISED AS WELL.
I DON'T WANT TO DIE.
I DON'T WANT TO DIE, LIKE MY SISTER.
I AM SCARED.

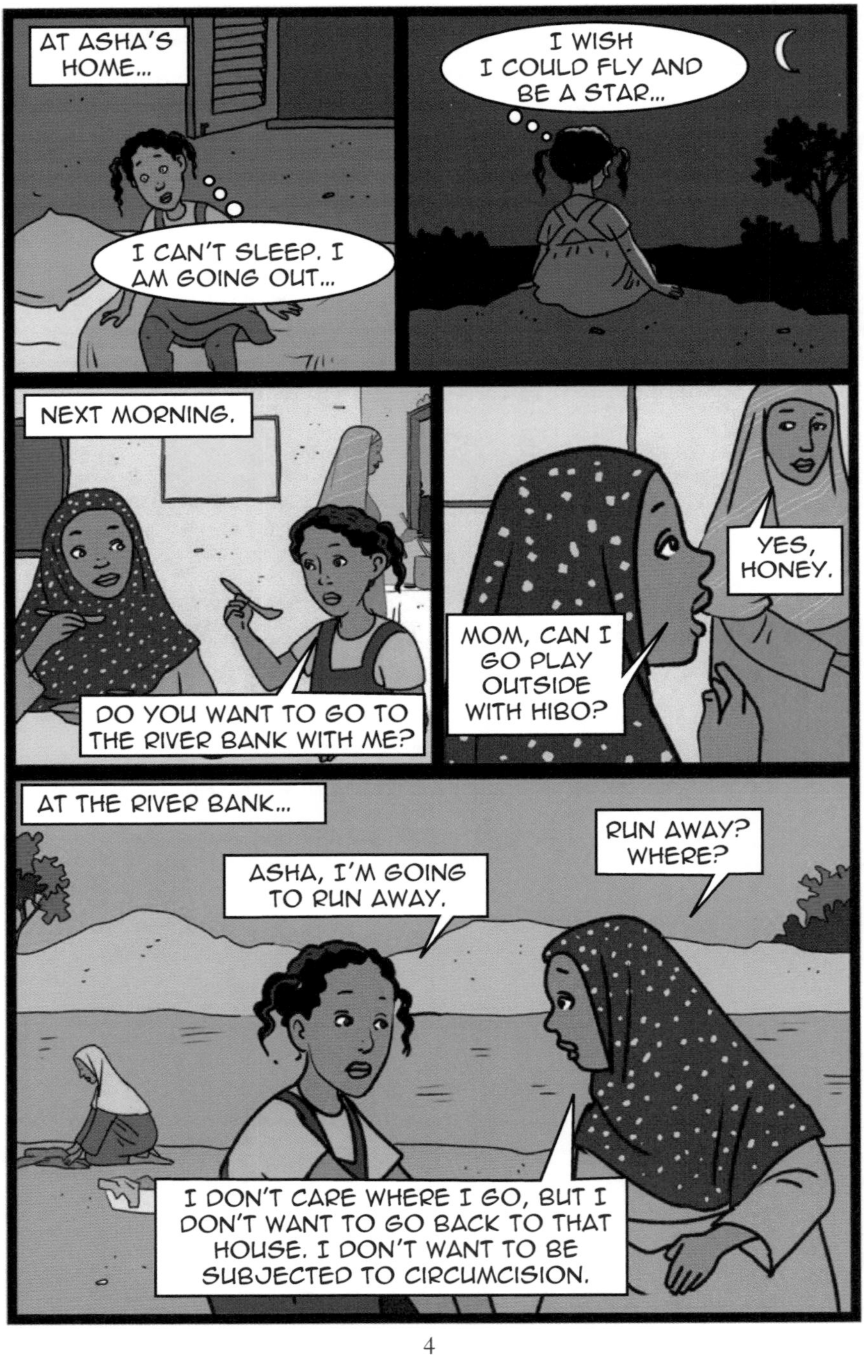
AT ASHA'S HOME...
I CAN'T SLEEP. I AM GOING OUT...
I WISH I COULD FLY AND BE A STAR...
NEXT MORNING.
DO YOU WANT TO GO TO THE RIVER BANK WITH ME?
MOM, CAN I GO PLAY OUTSIDE WITH HIBO?
YES, HONEY.
AT THE RIVER BANK...
ASHA, I'M GOING TO RUN AWAY.
RUN AWAY? WHERE?
I DON'T CARE WHERE I GO, BUT I DON'T WANT TO GO BACK TO THAT HOUSE. I DON'T WANT TO BE SUBJECTED TO CIRCUMCISION.

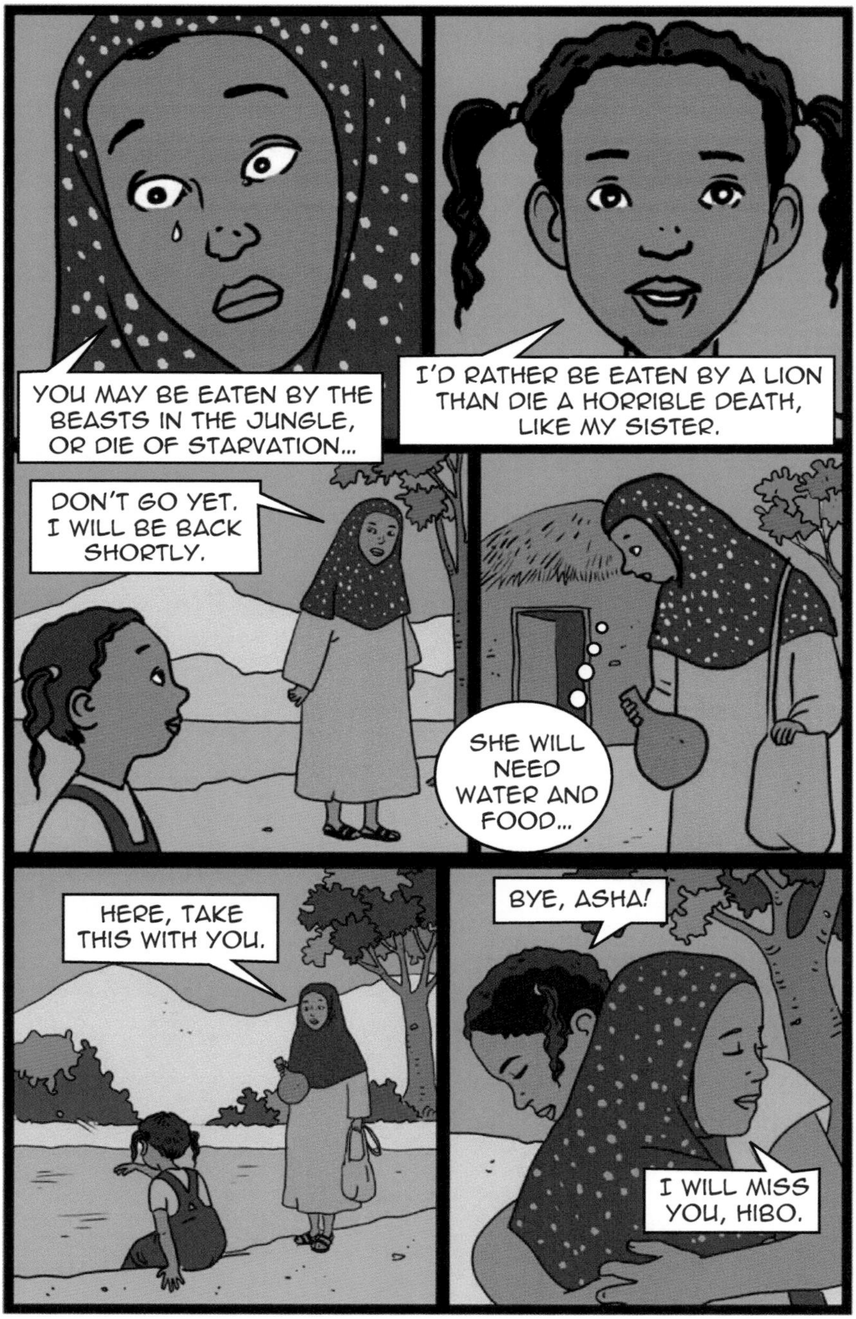
YOU MAY BE EATEN BY THE BEASTS IN THE JUNGLE, OR DIE OF STARVATION...
I'D RATHER BE EATEN BY A LION THAN DIE A HORRIBLE DEATH, LIKE MY SISTER.
DON'T GO YET. I WILL BE BACK SHORTLY.
SHE WILL NEED WATER AND FOOD...
HERE, TAKE THIS WITH YOU.
BYE, ASHA!
I WILL MISS YOU, HIBO.

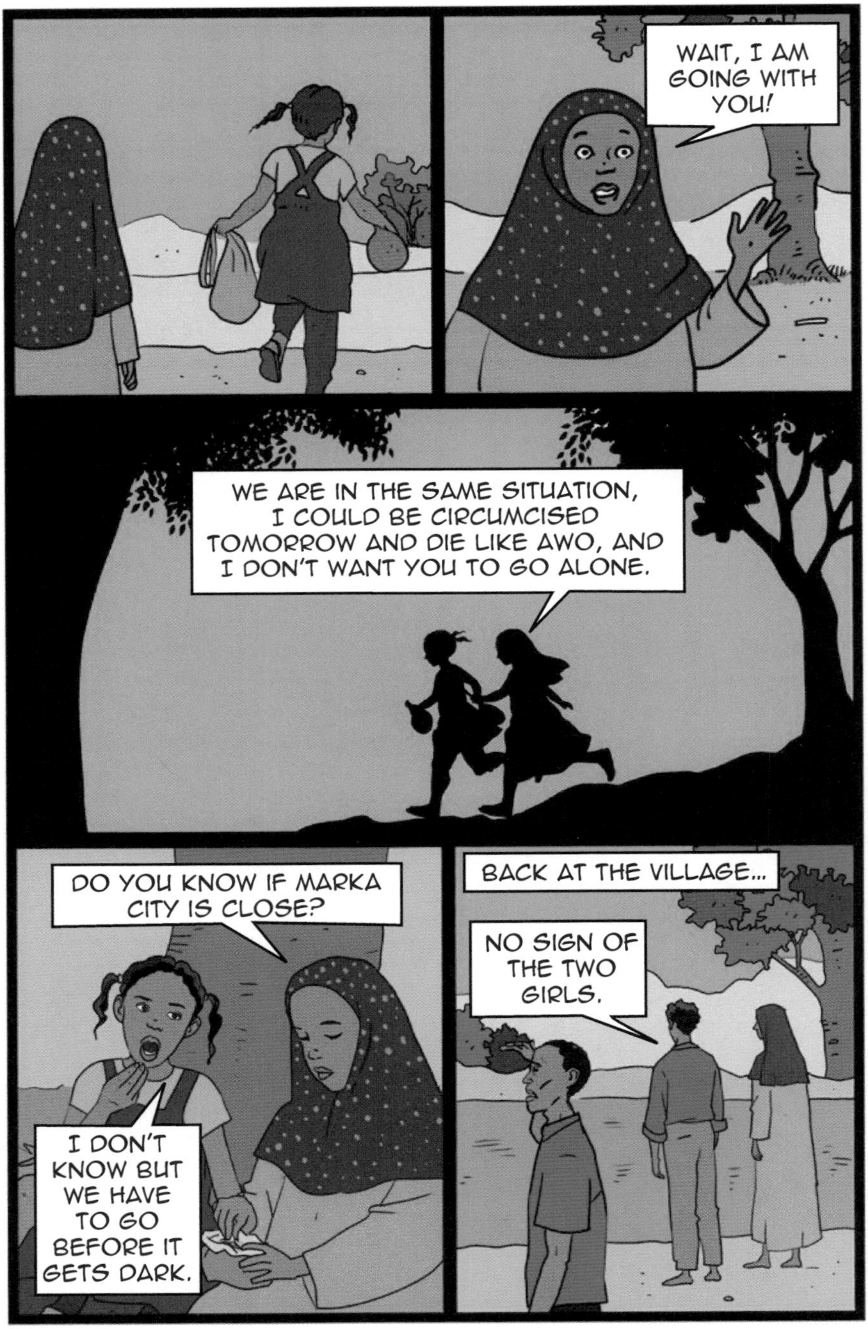
WAIT, I AM GOING WITH YOU!
WE ARE IN THE SAME SITUATION, I COULD BE CIRCUMCISED TOMORROW AND DIE LIKE AWO, AND I DON'T WANT YOU TO GO ALONE.
DO YOU KNOW IF MARKA CITY IS CLOSE?
I DON'T KNOW BUT WE HAVE TO GO BEFORE IT GETS DARK.
BACK AT THE VILLAGE...
NO SIGN OF THE TWO GIRLS.

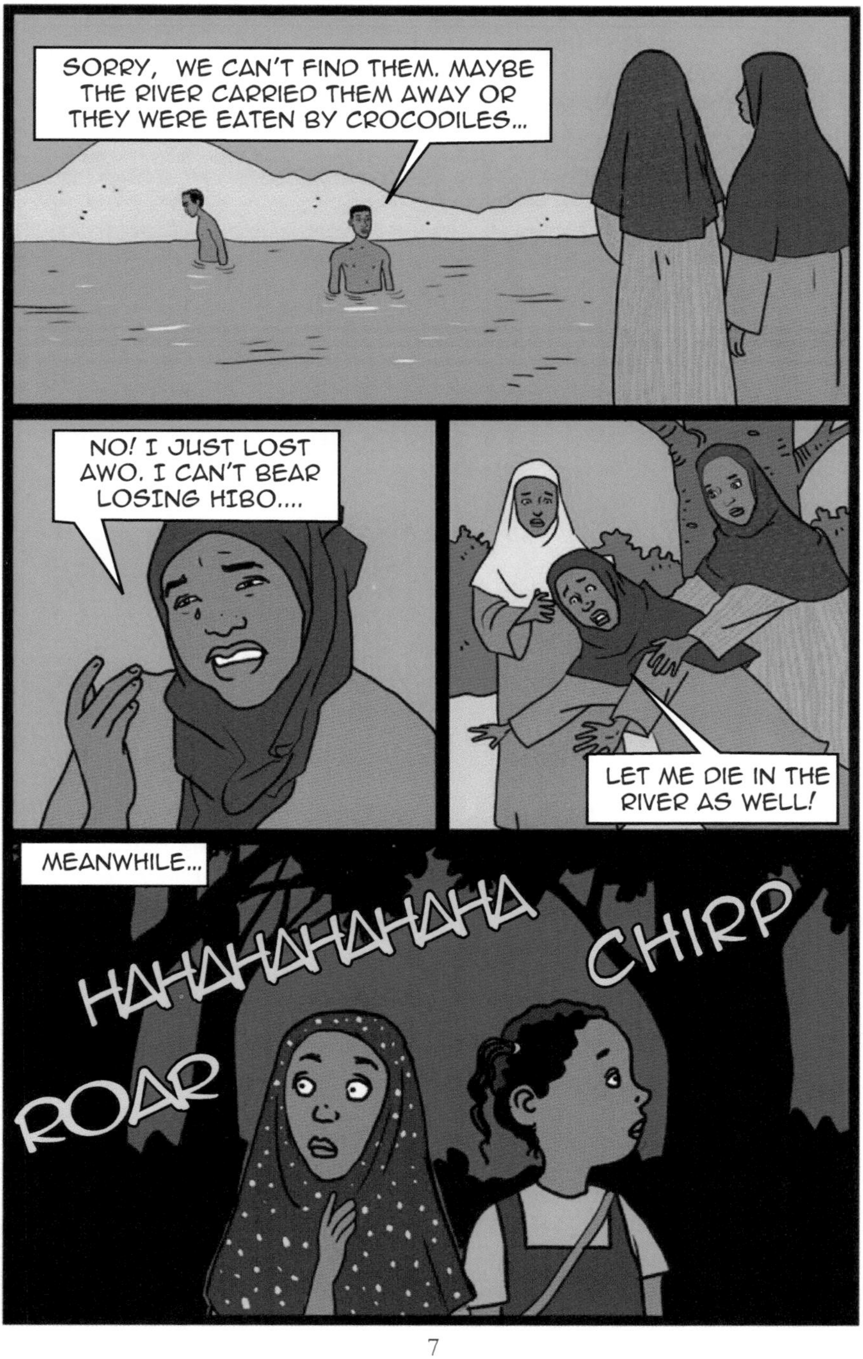
SORRY, WE CAN'T FIND THEM. MAYBE THE RIVER CARRIED THEM AWAY OR THEY WERE EATEN BY CROCODILES...
NO! I JUST LOST AWO. I CAN'T BEAR LOSING HIBO....
LET ME DIE IN THE RIVER AS WELL!
MEANWHILE...
HAHAHAHAHAHA
CHIRP
ROAR

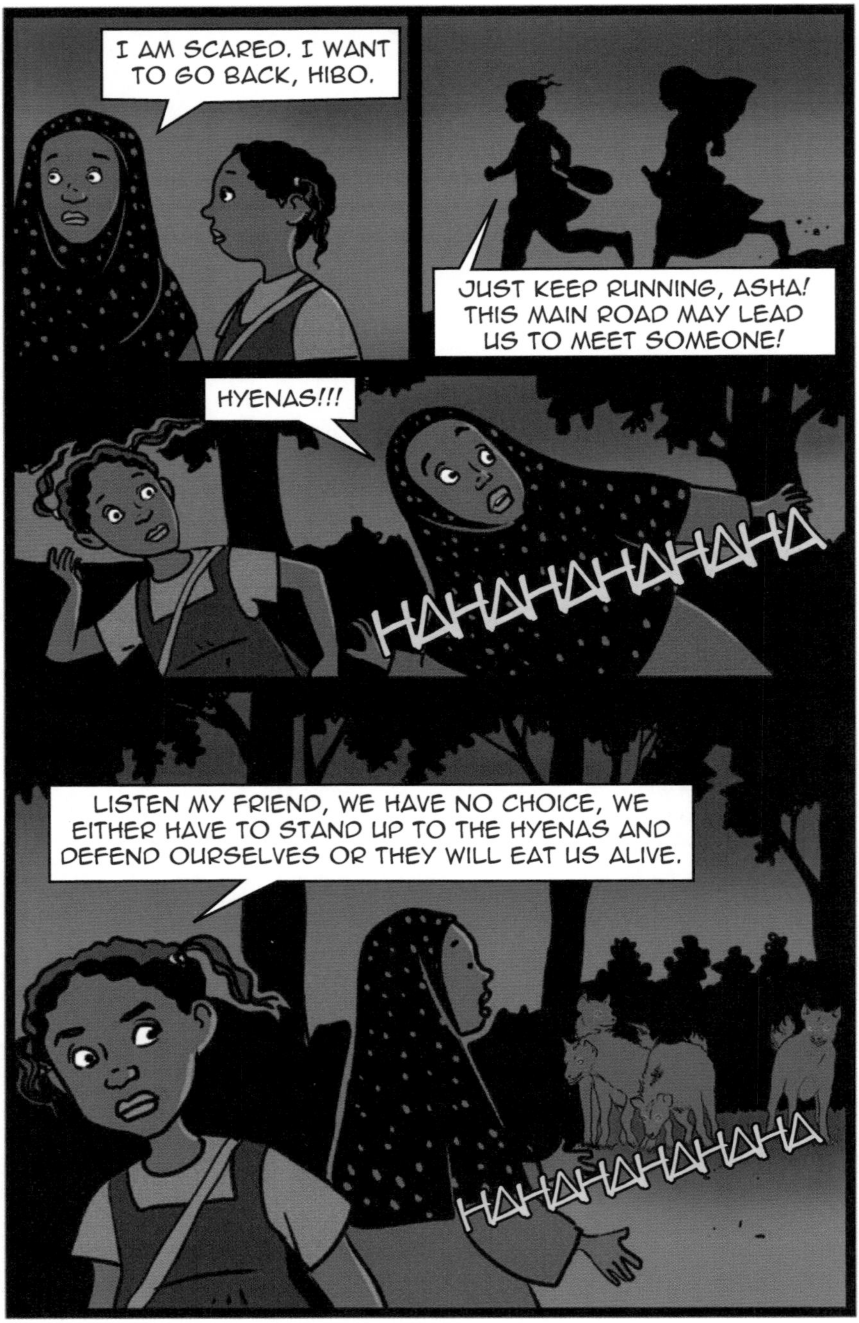
I AM SCARED. I WANT TO GO BACK, HIBO.
JUST KEEP RUNNING, ASHA! THIS MAIN ROAD MAY LEAD US TO MEET SOMEONE!
HYENAS!!!
HAHAHAHAHAHAHAHA
LISTEN MY FRIEND, WE HAVE NO CHOICE, WE EITHER HAVE TO STAND UP TO THE HYENAS AND DEFEND OURSELVES OR THEY WILL EAT US ALIVE.
HAHAHAHAHAHAHAHA

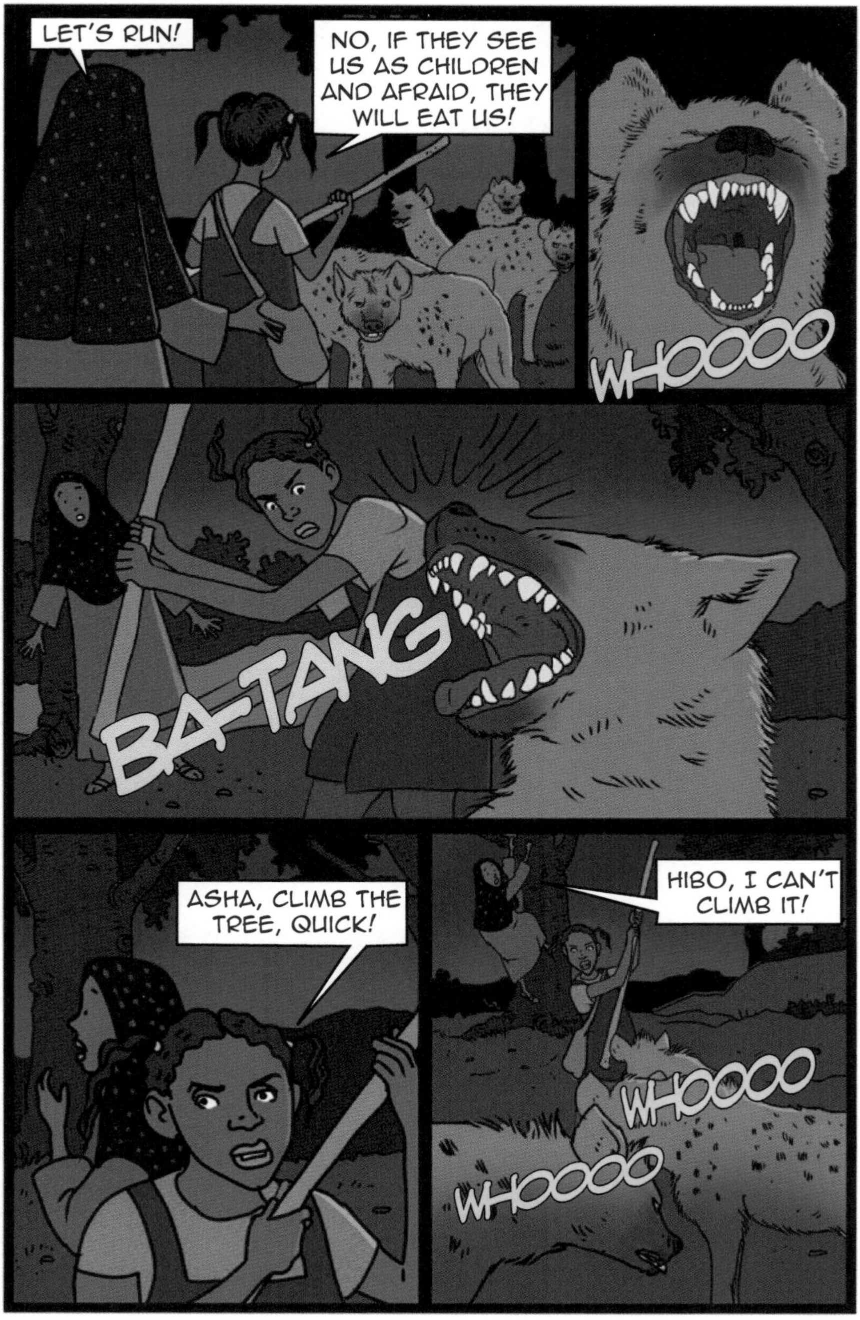
LET'S RUN!
NO, IF THEY SEE US AS CHILDREN AND AFRAID, THEY WILL EAT US!
WHOOOO
BA-TANG
ASHA, CLIMB THE TREE, QUICK!
HIBO, I CAN'T CLIMB IT!
WHOOOO
WHOOOO

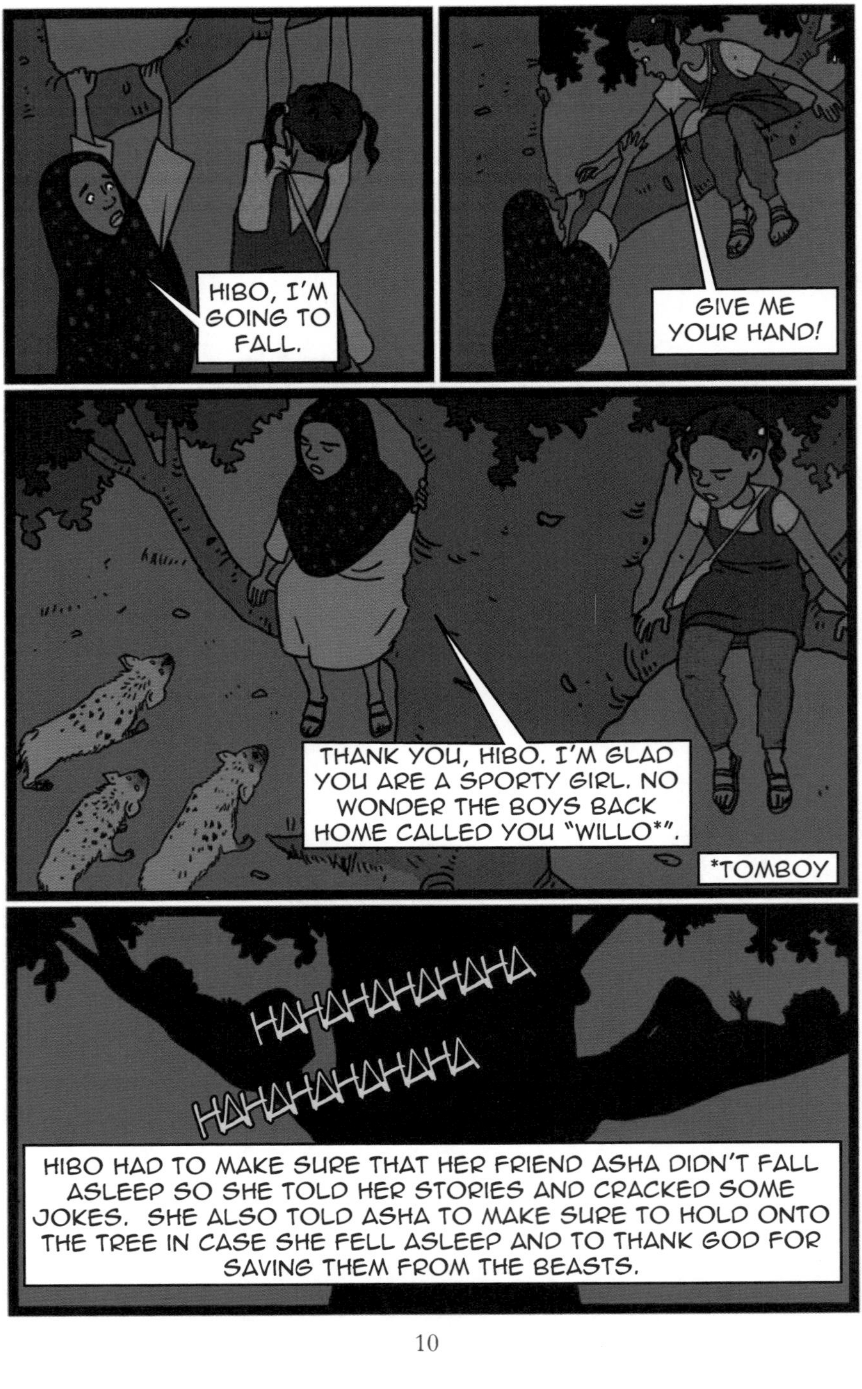
HIBO, I'M GOING TO FALL.
GIVE ME YOUR HAND!
THANK YOU, HIBO. I'M GLAD YOU ARE A SPORTY GIRL. NO WONDER THE BOYS BACK HOME CALLED YOU "WILLO*".
*TOMBOY
HAHAHAHAHAHA
HAHAHAHAHAHA
HIBO HAD TO MAKE SURE THAT HER FRIEND ASHA DIDN'T FALL ASLEEP SO SHE TOLD HER STORIES AND CRACKED SOME JOKES. SHE ALSO TOLD ASHA TO MAKE SURE TO HOLD ONTO THE TREE IN CASE SHE FELL ASLEEP AND TO THANK GOD FOR SAVING THEM FROM THE BEASTS.

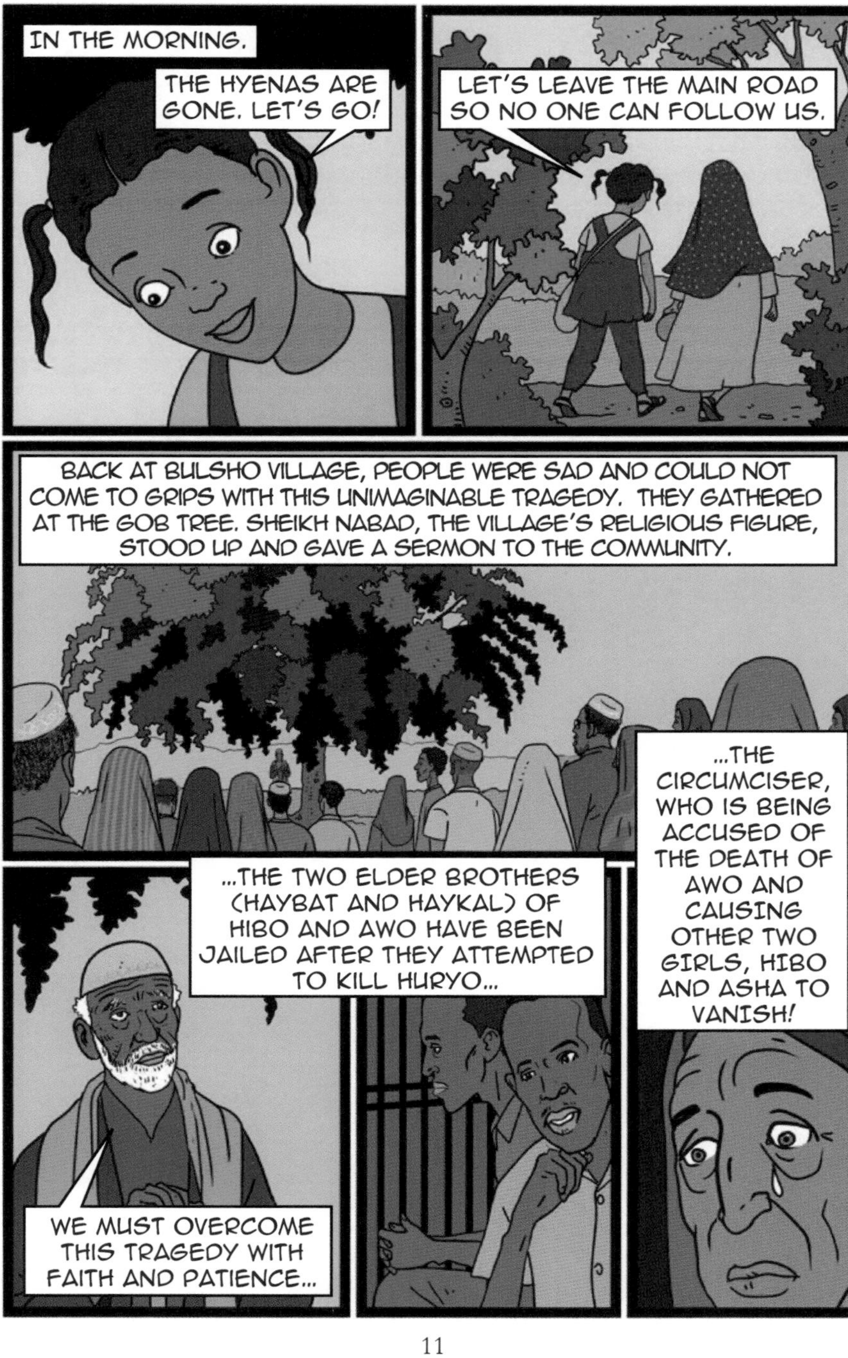
IN THE MORNING.
THE HYENAS ARE GONE. LET'S GO!
LET'S LEAVE THE MAIN ROAD SO NO ONE CAN FOLLOW US.
BACK AT BULSHO VILLAGE, PEOPLE WERE SAD AND COULD NOT COME TO GRIPS WITH THIS UNIMAGINABLE TRAGEDY. THEY GATHERED AT THE GOB TREE. SHEIKH NABAD, THE VILLAGE'S RELIGIOUS FIGURE, STOOD UP AND GAVE A SERMON TO THE COMMUNITY.
WE MUST OVERCOME THIS TRAGEDY WITH FAITH AND PATIENCE...
...THE TWO ELDER BROTHERS (HAYBAT AND HAYKAL) OF HIBO AND AWO HAVE BEEN JAILED AFTER THEY ATTEMPTED TO KILL HURYO...
...THE CIRCUMCISER, WHO IS BEING ACCUSED OF THE DEATH OF AWO AND CAUSING OTHER TWO GIRLS, HIBO AND ASHA TO VANISH!

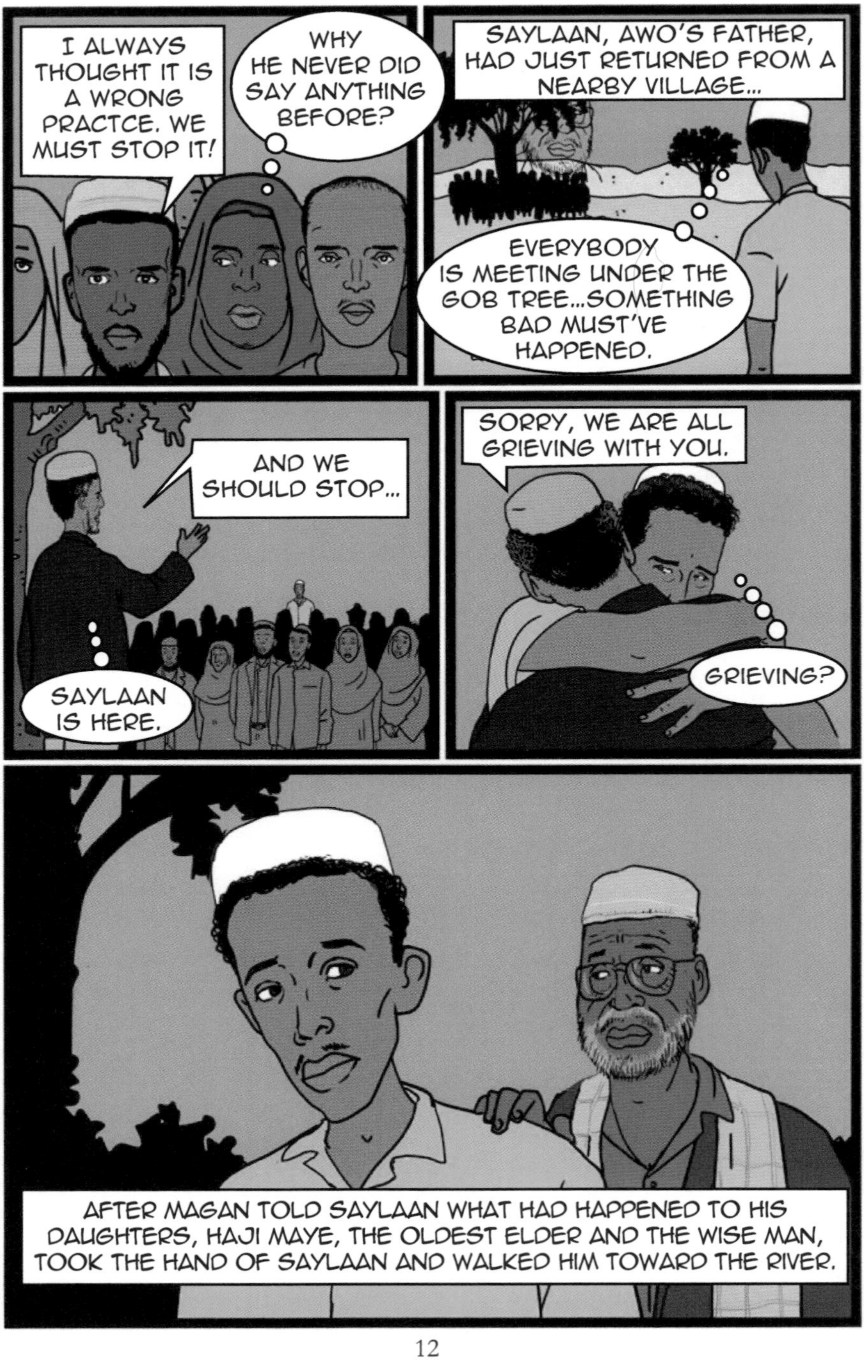
I ALWAYS THOUGHT IT IS A WRONG PRACTCE. WE MUST STOP IT!
WHY HE NEVER DID SAY ANYTHING BEFORE?
SAYLAAN, AWO'S FATHER, HAD JUST RETURNED FROM A NEARBY VILLAGE...
EVERYBODY IS MEETING UNDER THE GOB TREE...SOMETHING BAD MUST'VE HAPPENED.
AND WE SHOULD STOP...
SAYLAAN IS HERE.
SORRY, WE ARE ALL GRIEVING WITH YOU.
GRIEVING?
AFTER MAGAN TOLD SAYLAAN WHAT HAD HAPPENED TO HIS DAUGHTERS, HAJI MAYE, THE OLDEST ELDER AND THE WISE MAN, TOOK THE HAND OF SAYLAAN AND WALKED HIM TOWARD THE RIVER.

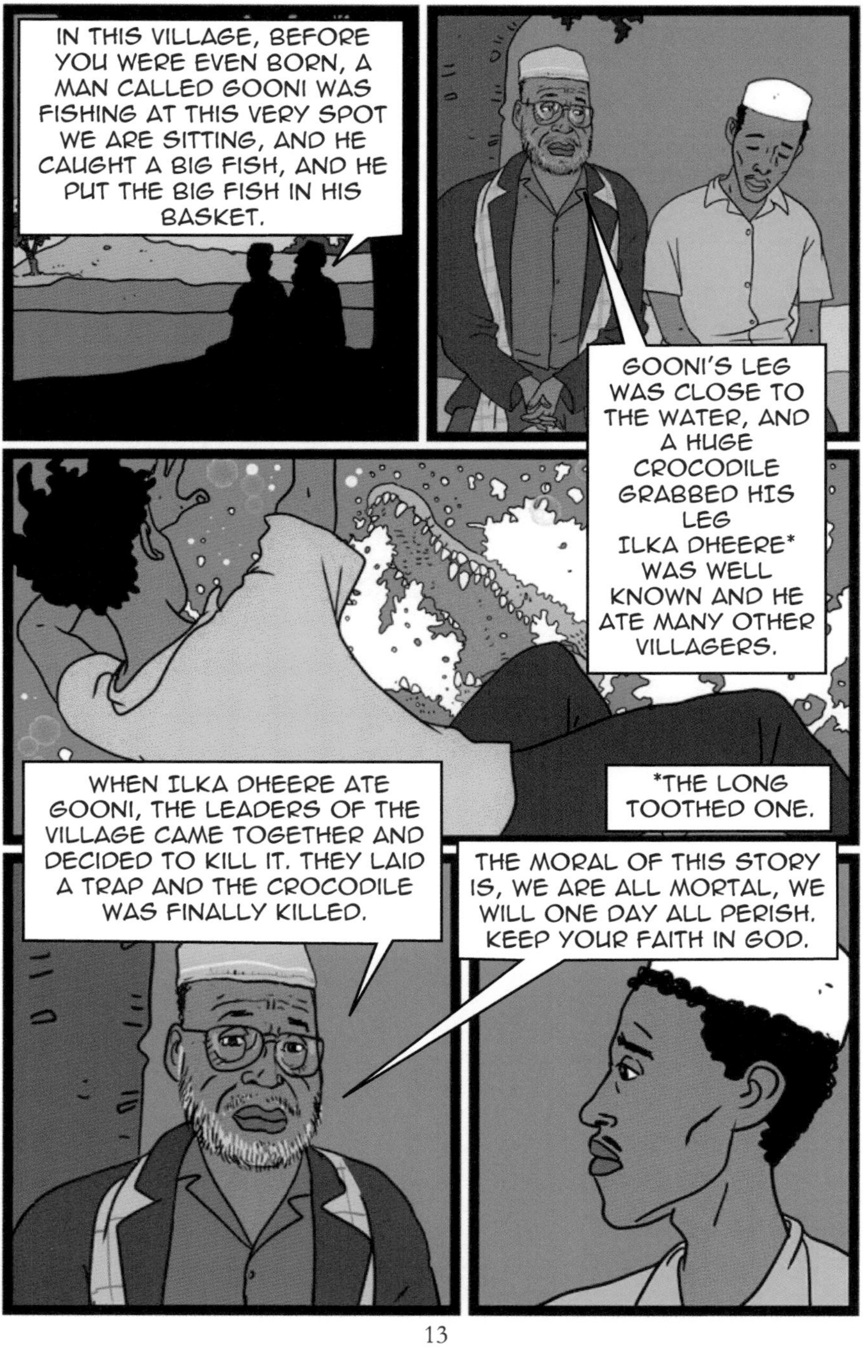
IN THIS VILLAGE, BEFORE YOU WERE EVEN BORN, A MAN CALLED GOONI WAS FISHING AT THIS VERY SPOT WE ARE SITTING, AND HE CAUGHT A BIG FISH, AND HE PUT THE BIG FISH IN HIS BASKET.
GOONI'S LEG WAS CLOSE TO THE WATER, AND A HUGE CROCODILE GRABBED HIS LEG
ILKA DHEERE* WAS WELL KNOWN AND HE ATE MANY OTHER VILLAGERS.
*THE LONG TOOTHED ONE.
WHEN ILKA DHEERE ATE GOONI, THE LEADERS OF THE VILLAGE CAME TOGETHER AND DECIDED TO KILL IT. THEY LAID A TRAP AND THE CROCODILE WAS FINALLY KILLED.
THE MORAL OF THIS STORY IS, WE ARE ALL MORTAL, WE WILL ONE DAY ALL PERISH. KEEP YOUR FAITH IN GOD.

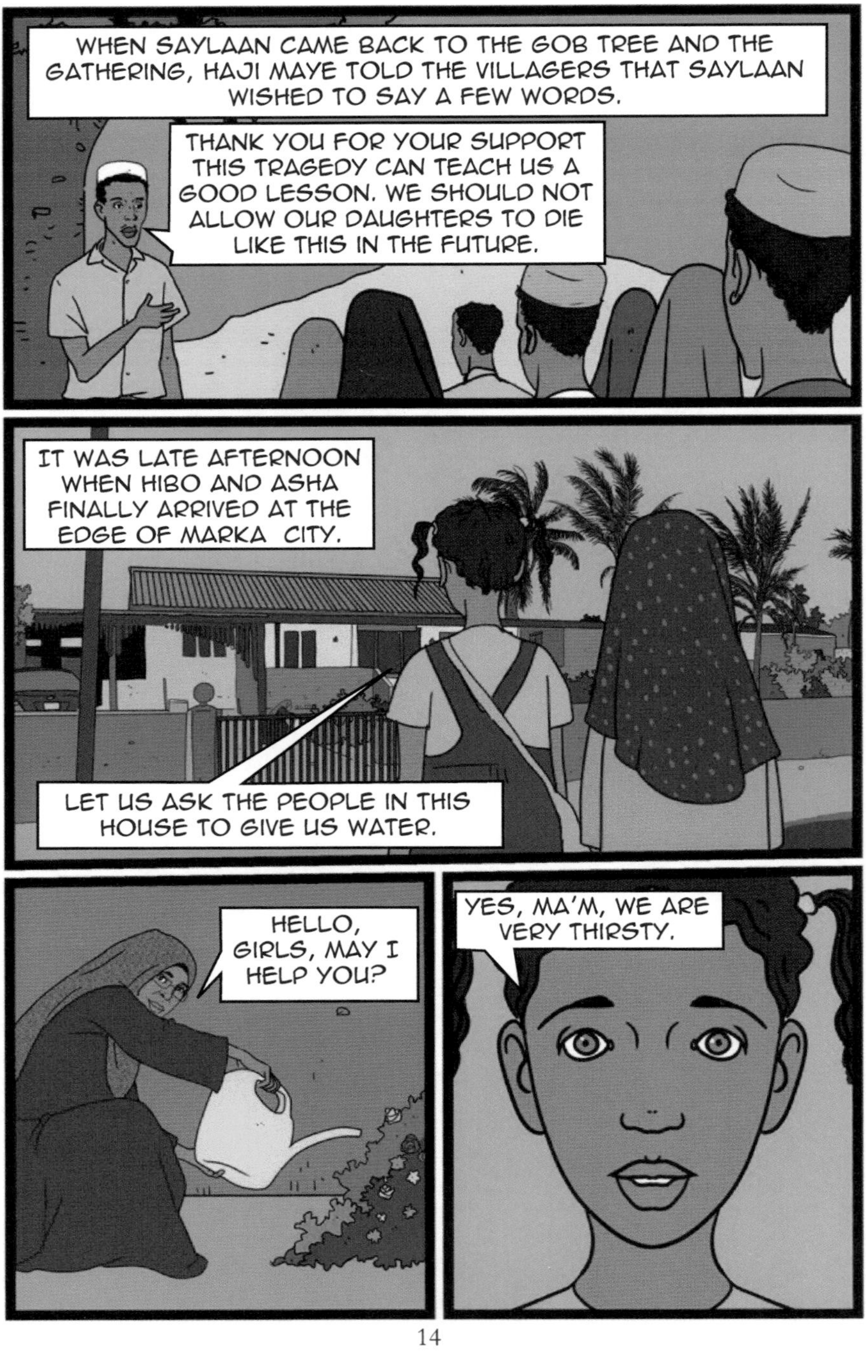
WHEN SAYLAAN CAME BACK TO THE GOB TREE AND THE GATHERING, HAJI MAYE TOLD THE VILLAGERS THAT SAYLAAN WISHED TO SAY A FEW WORDS.
THANK YOU FOR YOUR SUPPORT THIS TRAGEDY CAN TEACH US A GOOD LESSON. WE SHOULD NOT ALLOW OUR DAUGHTERS TO DIE LIKE THIS IN THE FUTURE.
IT WAS LATE AFTERNOON WHEN HIBO AND ASHA FINALLY ARRIVED AT THE EDGE OF MARKA CITY.
LET US ASK THE PEOPLE IN THIS HOUSE TO GIVE US WATER.
HELLO, GIRLS, MAY I HELP YOU?
YES, MA'M, WE ARE VERY THIRSTY.

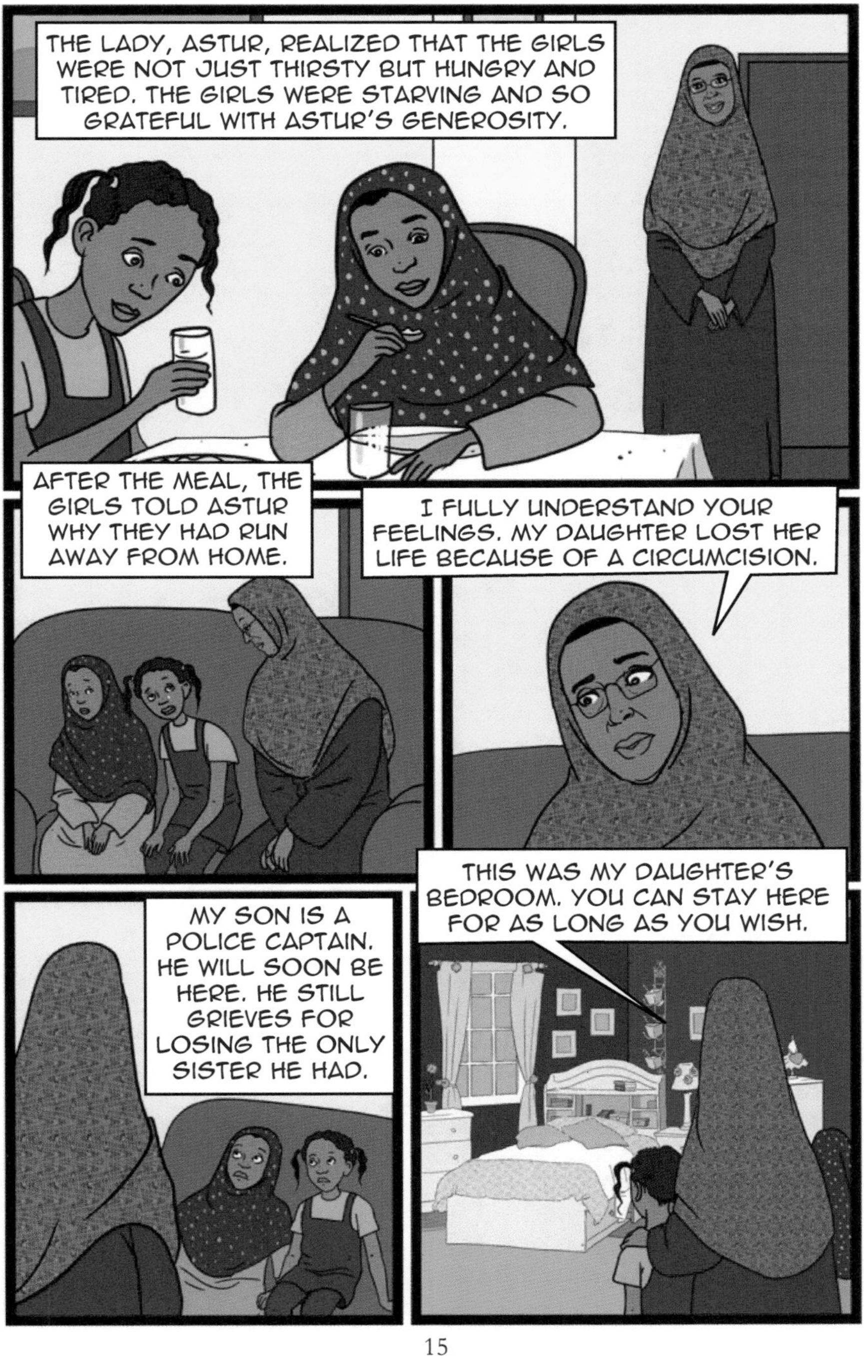
THE LADY, ASTUR, REALIZED THAT THE GIRLS WERE NOT JUST THIRSTY BUT HUNGRY AND TIRED. THE GIRLS WERE STARVING AND SO GRATEFUL WITH ASTUR'S GENEROSITY.
AFTER THE MEAL, THE GIRLS TOLD ASTUR WHY THEY HAD RUN AWAY FROM HOME.
I FULLY UNDERSTAND YOUR FEELINGS. MY DAUGHTER LOST HER LIFE BECAUSE OF A CIRCUMCISION.
MY SON IS A POLICE CAPTAIN. HE WILL SOON BE HERE. HE STILL GRIEVES FOR LOSING THE ONLY SISTER HE HAD.
THIS WAS MY DAUGHTER'S BEDROOM. YOU CAN STAY HERE FOR AS LONG AS YOU WISH.

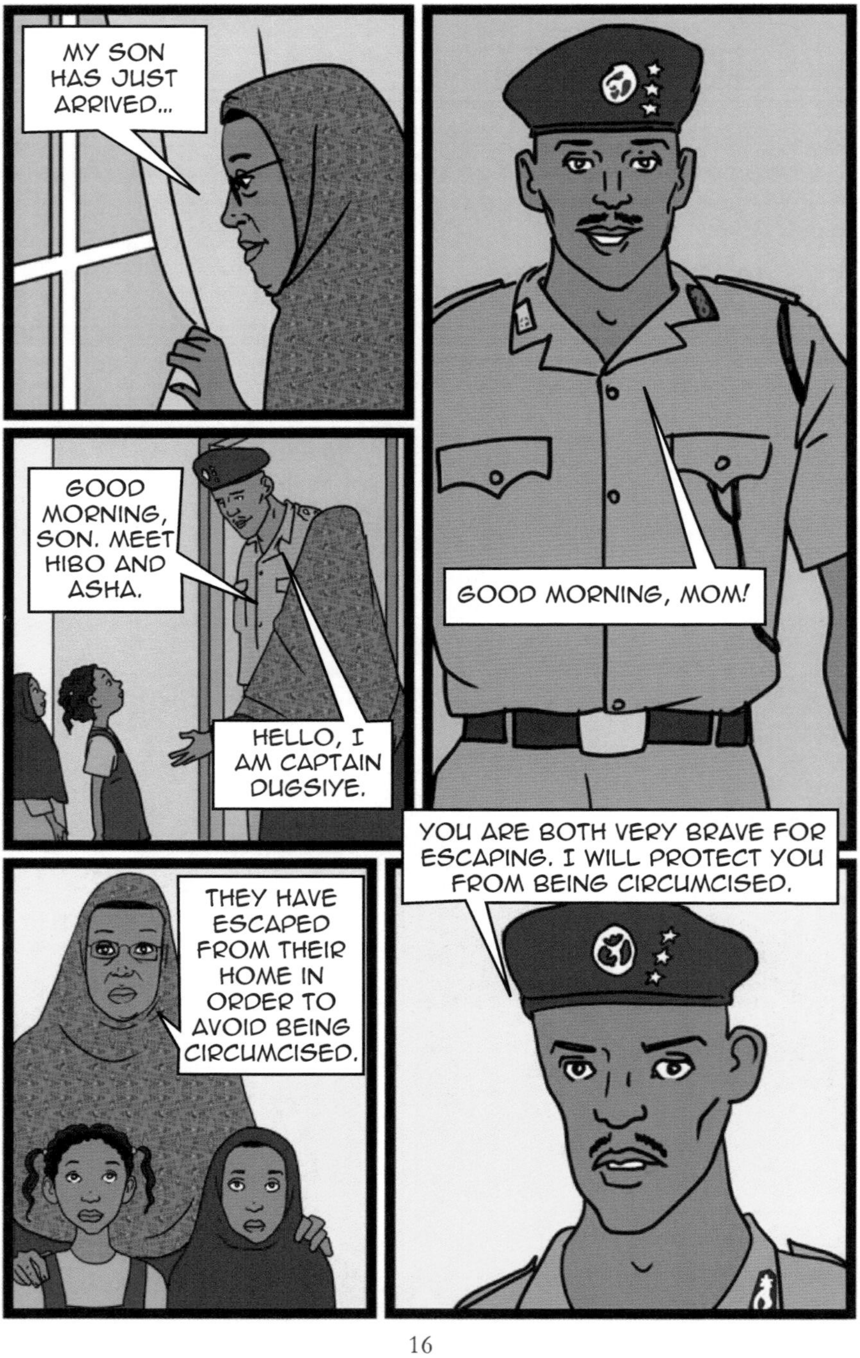
MY SON HAS JUST ARRIVED...
GOOD MORNING, MOM!
GOOD MORNING, SON. MEET HIBO AND ASHA.
HELLO, I AM CAPTAIN DUGSIYE.
THEY HAVE ESCAPED FROM THEIR HOME IN ORDER TO AVOID BEING CIRCUMCISED.
YOU ARE BOTH VERY BRAVE FOR ESCAPING. I WILL PROTECT YOU FROM BEING CIRCUMCISED.

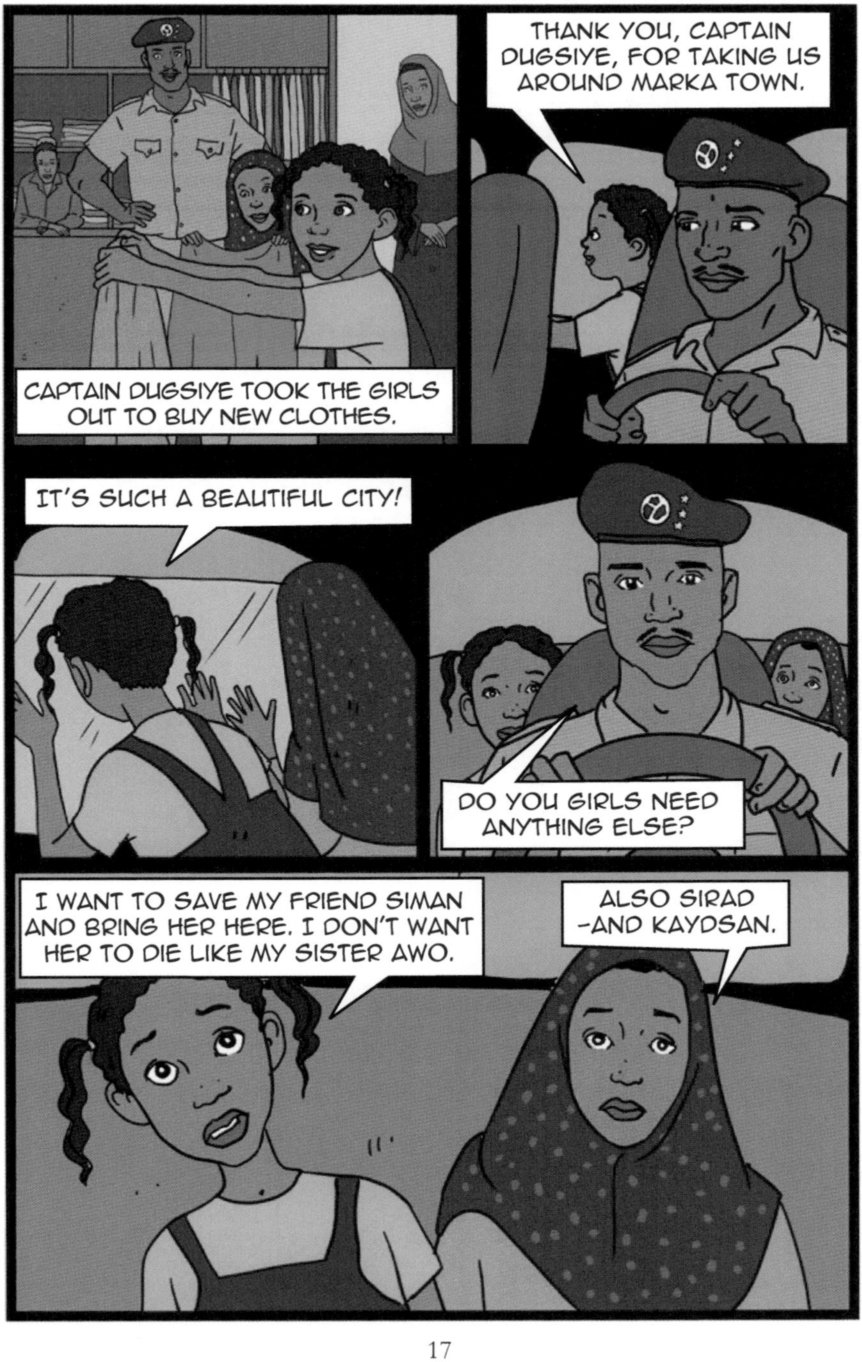
CAPTAIN DUGSIYE TOOK THE GIRLS OUT TO BUY NEW CLOTHES.
THANK YOU, CAPTAIN DUGSIYE, FOR TAKING US AROUND MARKA TOWN.
IT'S SUCH A BEAUTIFUL CITY!
DO YOU GIRLS NEED ANYTHING ELSE?
I WANT TO SAVE MY FRIEND SIMAN AND BRING HER HERE. I DON'T WANT HER TO DIE LIKE MY SISTER AWO.
ALSO SIRAD -AND KAYDSAN.

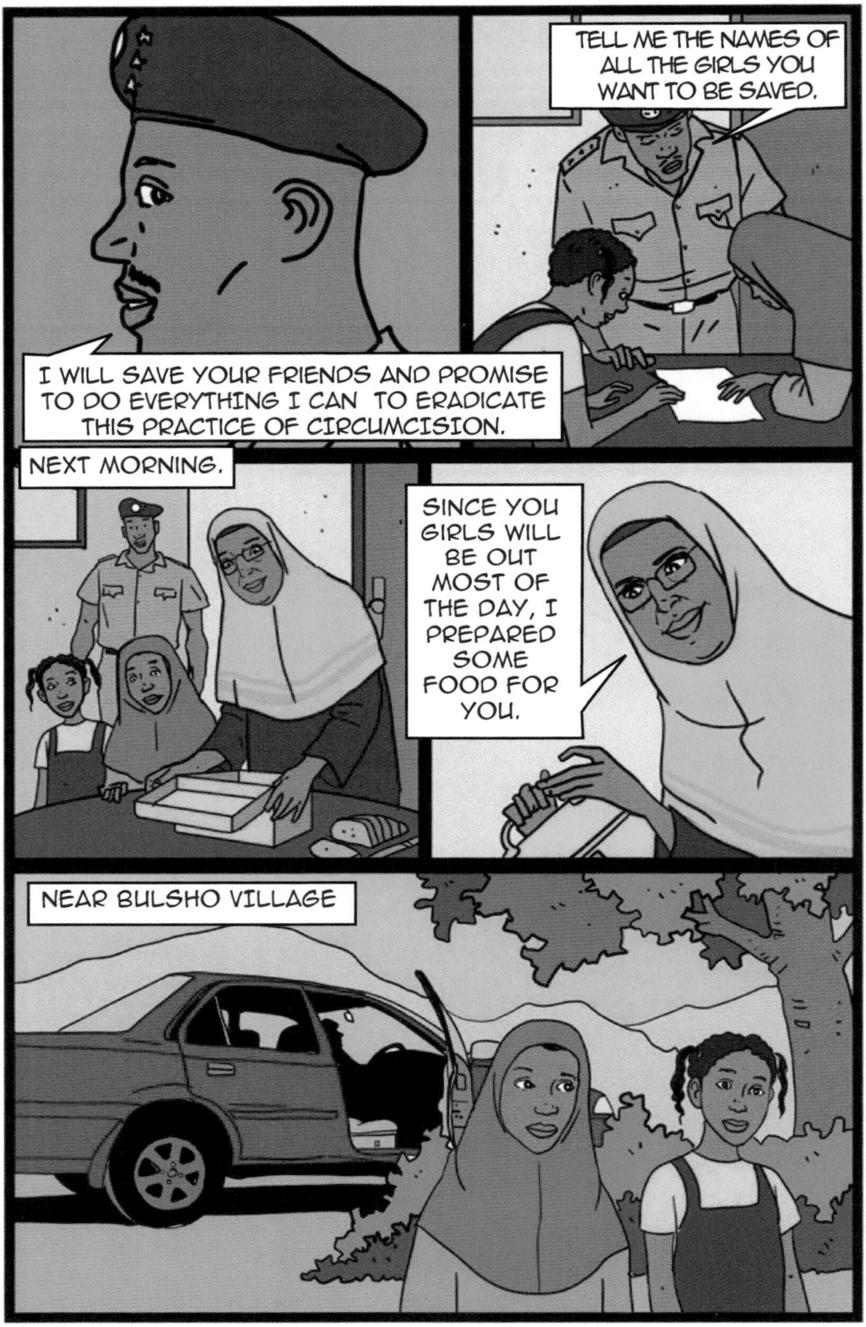
I WILL SAVE YOUR FRIENDS AND PROMISE TO DO EVERYTHING I CAN TO ERADICATE THIS PRACTICE OF CIRCUMCISION.
TELL ME THE NAMES OF ALL THE GIRLS YOU WANT TO BE SAVED.
NEXT MORNING.
SINCE YOU GIRLS WILL BE OUT MOST OF THE DAY, I PREPARED SOME FOOD FOR YOU.
NEAR BULSHO VILLAGE

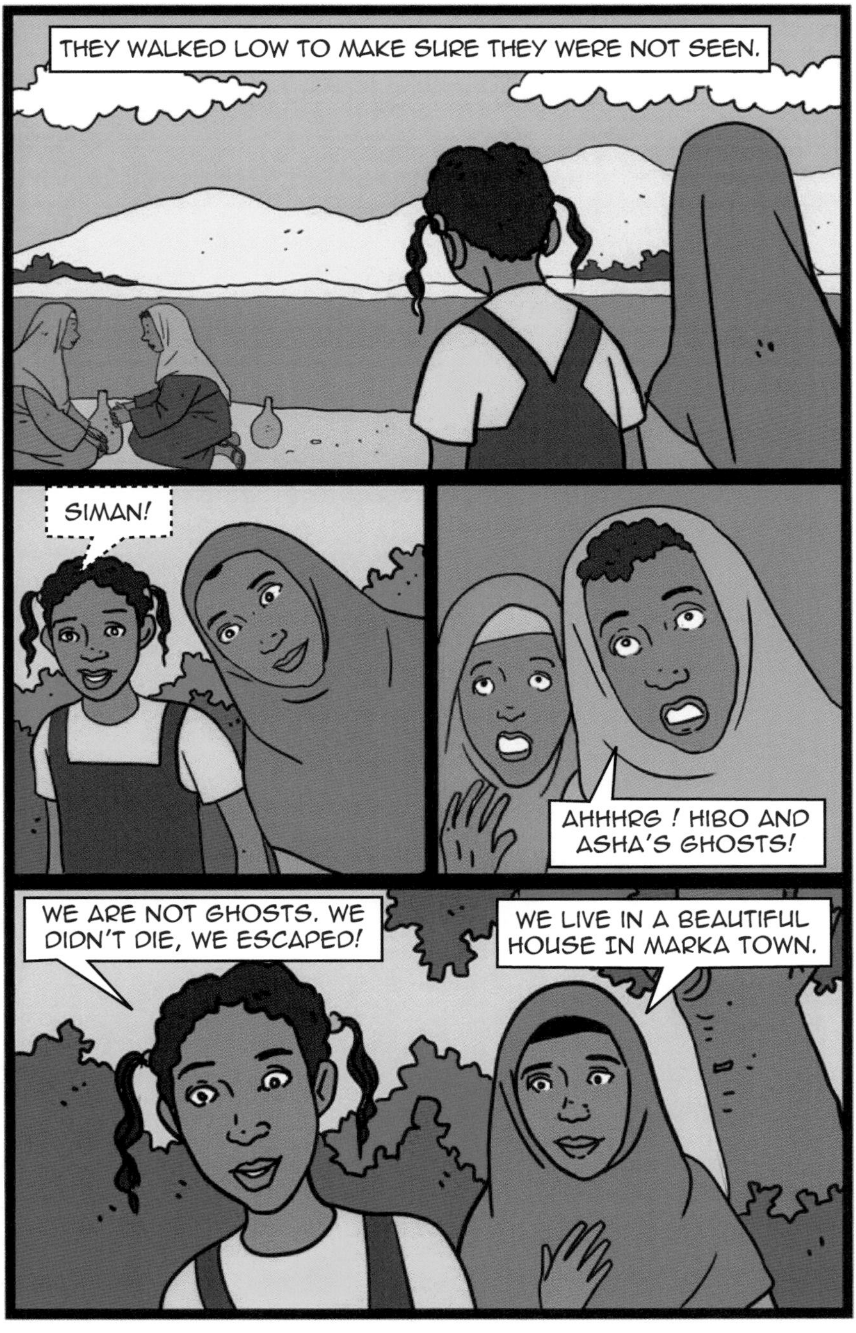
THEY WALKED LOW TO MAKE SURE THEY WERE NOT SEEN.
SIMAN!
AHHHRG ! HIBO AND ASHA'S GHOSTS!
WE ARE NOT GHOSTS. WE DIDN'T DIE, WE ESCAPED!
WE LIVE IN A BEAUTIFUL HOUSE IN MARKA TOWN.

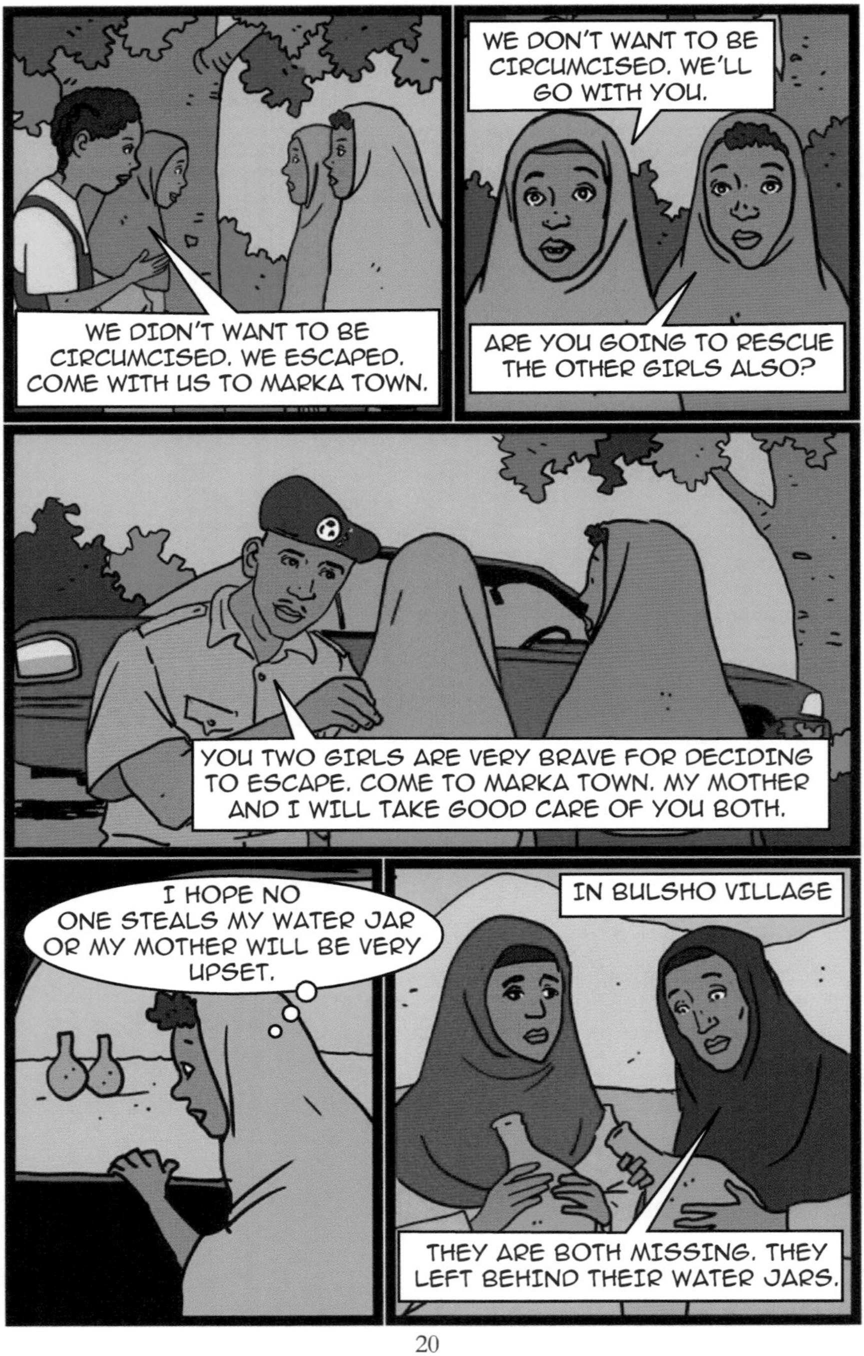
WE DIDN'T WANT TO BE CIRCUMCISED. WE ESCAPED. COME WITH US TO MARKA TOWN.
WE DON'T WANT TO BE CIRCUMCISED. WE'LL GO WITH YOU.
ARE YOU GOING TO RESCUE THE OTHER GIRLS ALSO?
YOU TWO GIRLS ARE VERY BRAVE FOR DECIDING TO ESCAPE. COME TO MARKA TOWN. MY MOTHER AND I WILL TAKE GOOD CARE OF YOU BOTH.
I HOPE NO ONE STEALS MY WATER JAR OR MY MOTHER WILL BE VERY UPSET.
IN BULSHO VILLAGE
THEY ARE BOTH MISSING. THEY LEFT BEHIND THEIR WATER JARS.

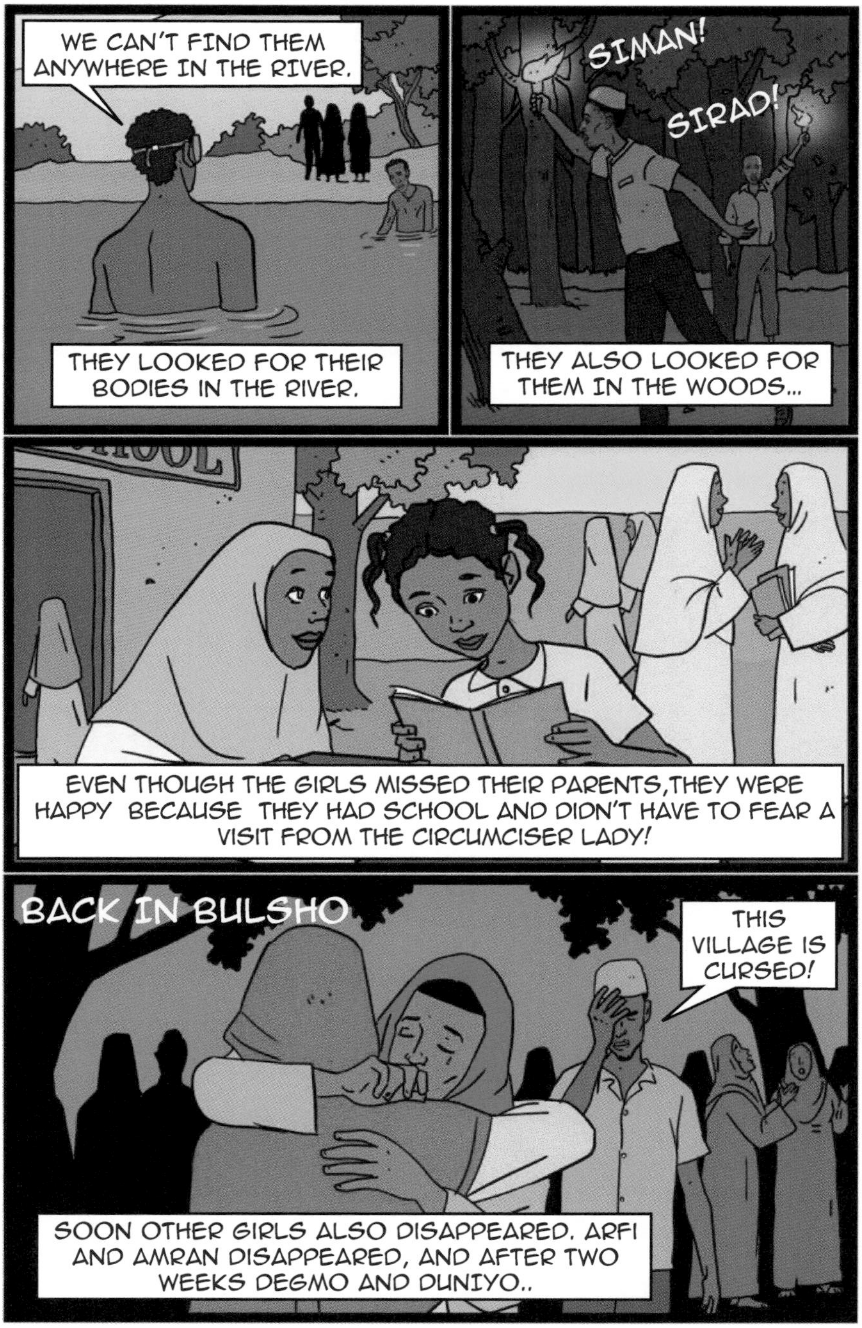
WE CAN'T FIND THEM ANYWHERE IN THE RIVER.
THEY LOOKED FOR THEIR BODIES IN THE RIVER.
SIMAN!
SIRAD!
THEY ALSO LOOKED FOR THEM IN THE WOODS...
EVEN THOUGH THE GIRLS MISSED THEIR PARENTS,THEY WERE HAPPY BECAUSE THEY HAD SCHOOL AND DIDN'T HAVE TO FEAR A VISIT FROM THE CIRCUMCISER LADY!
BACK IN BULSHO
THIS VILLAGE IS CURSED!
SOON OTHER GIRLS ALSO DISAPPEARED. ARFI AND AMRAN DISAPPEARED, AND AFTER TWO WEEKS DEGMO AND DUNIYO..

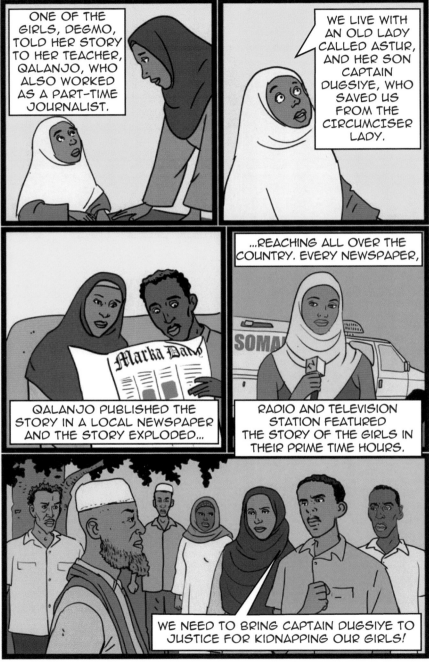

ONE OF THE GIRLS, DEGMO, TOLD HER STORY TO HER TEACHER, QALANJO, WHO ALSO WORKED AS A PART-TIME JOURNALIST.

WE LIVE WITH AN OLD LADY CALLED ASTUR, AND HER SON CAPTAIN DUGSIYE, WHO SAVED US FROM THE CIRCUMCISER LADY.

QALANJO PUBLISHED THE STORY IN A LOCAL NEWSPAPER AND THE STORY EXPLODED...

...REACHING ALL OVER THE COUNTRY. EVERY NEWSPAPER,

RADIO AND TELEVISION STATION FEATURED THE STORY OF THE GIRLS IN THEIR PRIME TIME HOURS.

WE NEED TO BRING CAPTAIN DUGSIYE TO JUSTICE FOR KIDNAPPING OUR GIRLS!

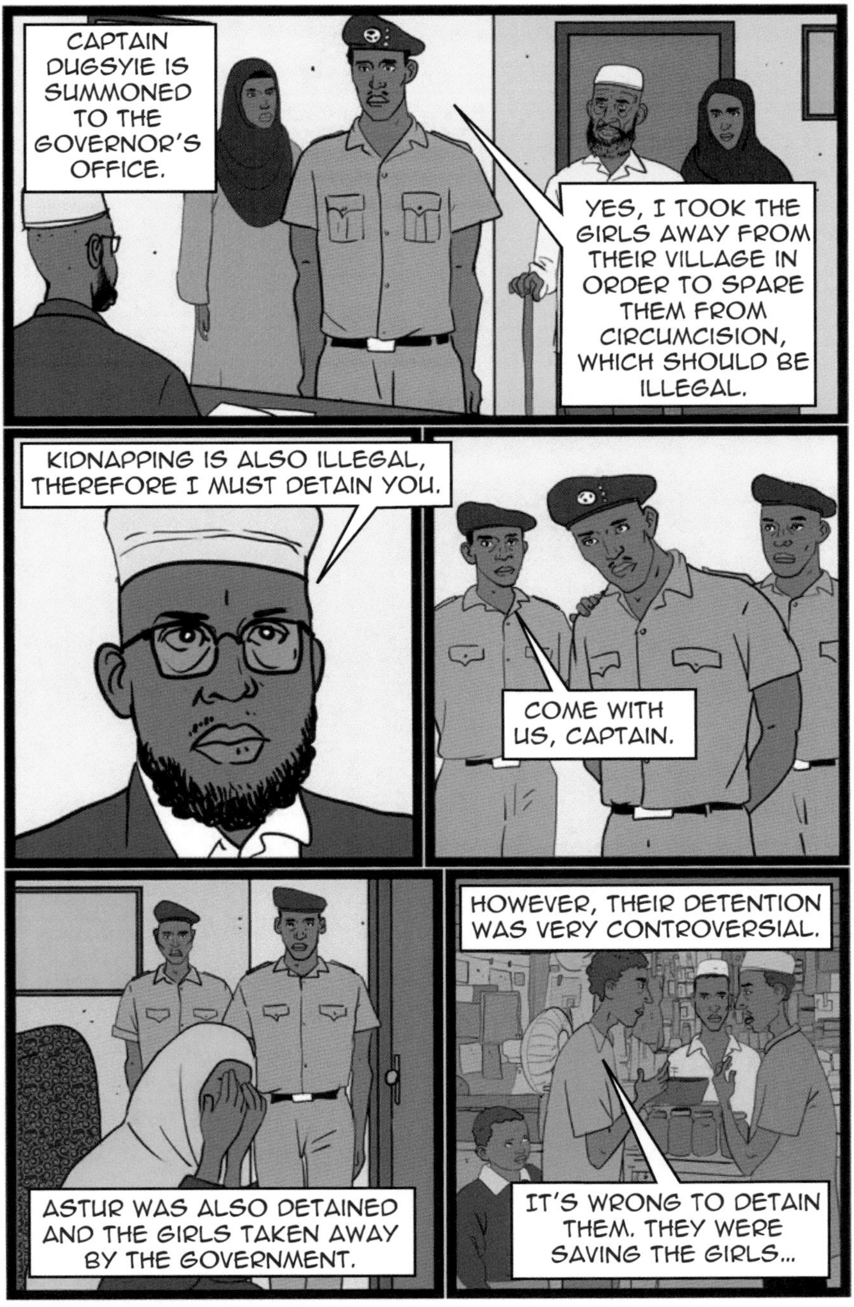
CAPTAIN DUGSYIE IS SUMMONED TO THE GOVERNOR'S OFFICE.
YES, I TOOK THE GIRLS AWAY FROM THEIR VILLAGE IN ORDER TO SPARE THEM FROM CIRCUMCISION, WHICH SHOULD BE ILLEGAL.
KIDNAPPING IS ALSO ILLEGAL, THEREFORE I MUST DETAIN YOU.
COME WITH US, CAPTAIN.
ASTUR WAS ALSO DETAINED AND THE GIRLS TAKEN AWAY BY THE GOVERNMENT.
HOWEVER, THEIR DETENTION WAS VERY CONTROVERSIAL.
IT'S WRONG TO DETAIN THEM. THEY WERE SAVING THE GIRLS...

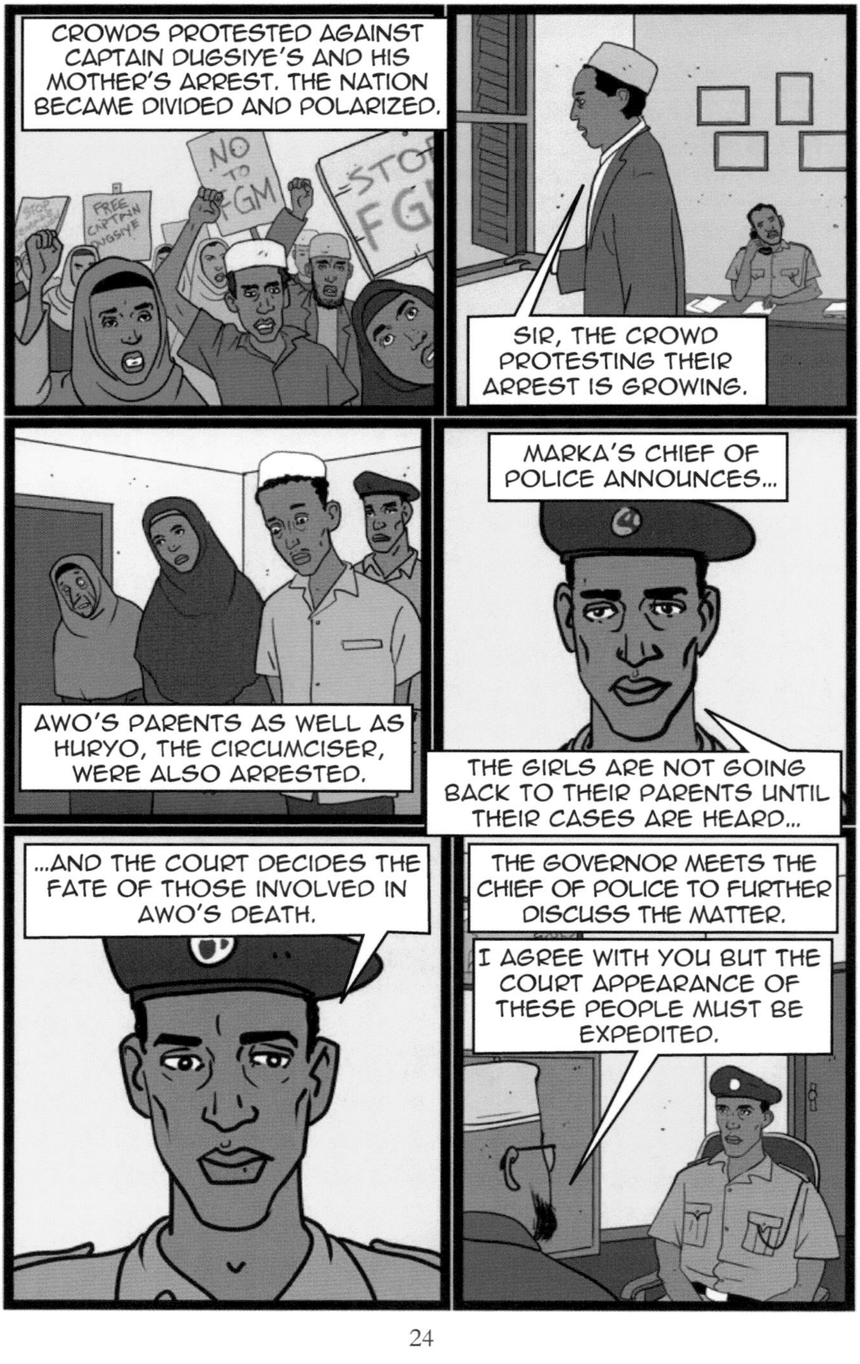
CROWDS PROTESTED AGAINST CAPTAIN DUGSIYE'S AND HIS MOTHER'S ARREST. THE NATION BECAME DIVIDED AND POLARIZED.
NO TO FGM
STOP FGM
FREE CAPTAIN DUGSIYE
SIR, THE CROWD PROTESTING THEIR ARREST IS GROWING.
AWO'S PARENTS AS WELL AS HURYO, THE CIRCUMCISER, WERE ALSO ARRESTED.
MARKA'S CHIEF OF POLICE ANNOUNCES...
THE GIRLS ARE NOT GOING BACK TO THEIR PARENTS UNTIL THEIR CASES ARE HEARD...
...AND THE COURT DECIDES THE FATE OF THOSE INVOLVED IN AWO'S DEATH.
THE GOVERNOR MEETS THE CHIEF OF POLICE TO FURTHER DISCUSS THE MATTER.
I AGREE WITH YOU BUT THE COURT APPEARANCE OF THESE PEOPLE MUST BE EXPEDITED.

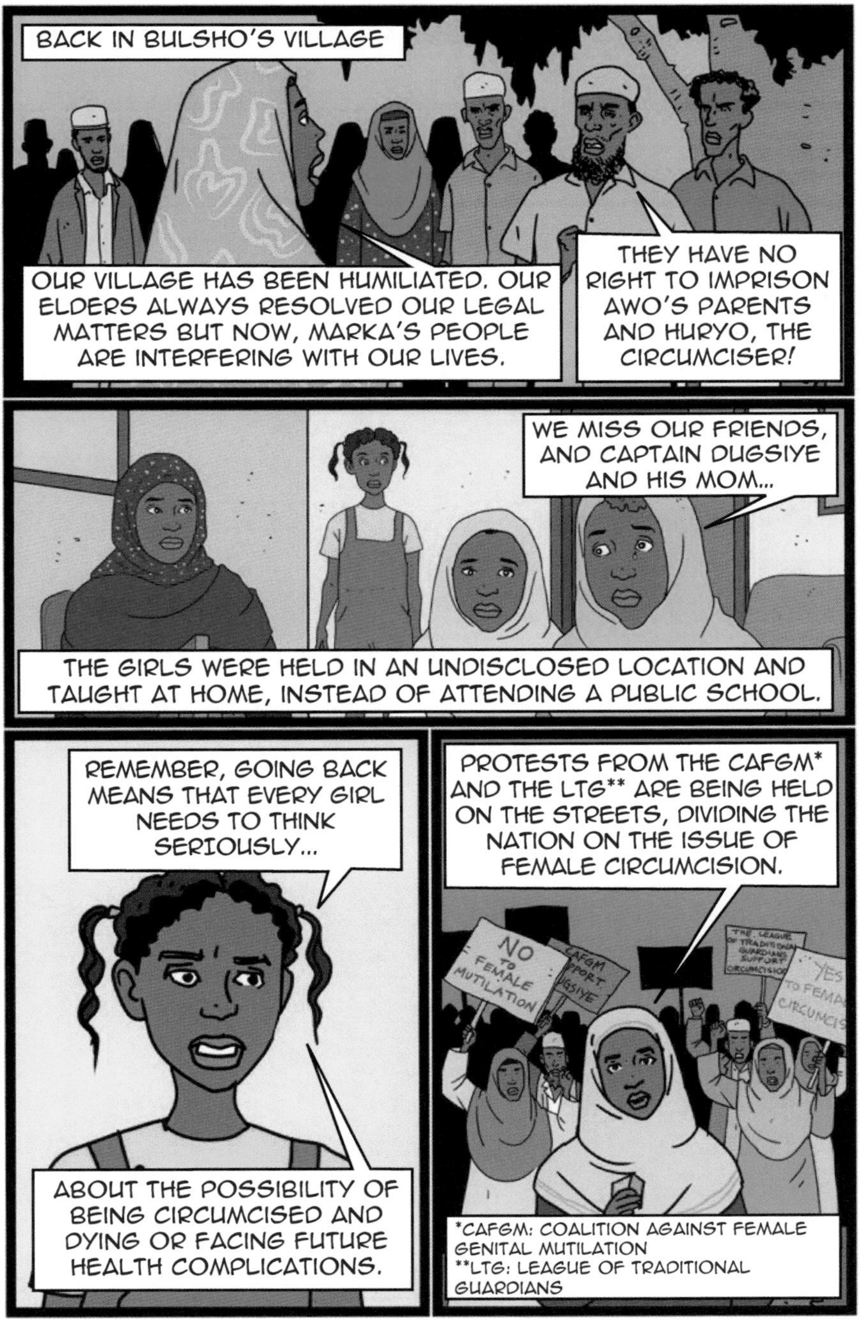
BACK IN BULSHO'S VILLAGE
OUR VILLAGE HAS BEEN HUMILIATED. OUR ELDERS ALWAYS RESOLVED OUR LEGAL MATTERS BUT NOW, MARKA'S PEOPLE ARE INTERFERING WITH OUR LIVES.
THEY HAVE NO RIGHT TO IMPRISON AWO'S PARENTS AND HURYO, THE CIRCUMCISER!
WE MISS OUR FRIENDS, AND CAPTAIN DUGSIYE AND HIS MOM...
THE GIRLS WERE HELD IN AN UNDISCLOSED LOCATION AND TAUGHT AT HOME, INSTEAD OF ATTENDING A PUBLIC SCHOOL.
REMEMBER, GOING BACK MEANS THAT EVERY GIRL NEEDS TO THINK SERIOUSLY...
ABOUT THE POSSIBILITY OF BEING CIRCUMCISED AND DYING OR FACING FUTURE HEALTH COMPLICATIONS.
PROTESTS FROM THE CAFGM* AND THE LTG** ARE BEING HELD ON THE STREETS, DIVIDING THE NATION ON THE ISSUE OF FEMALE CIRCUMCISION.
NO TO FEMALE MUTILATION
*CAFGM: COALITION AGAINST FEMALE GENITAL MUTILATION
**LTG: LEAGUE OF TRADITIONAL GUARDIANS

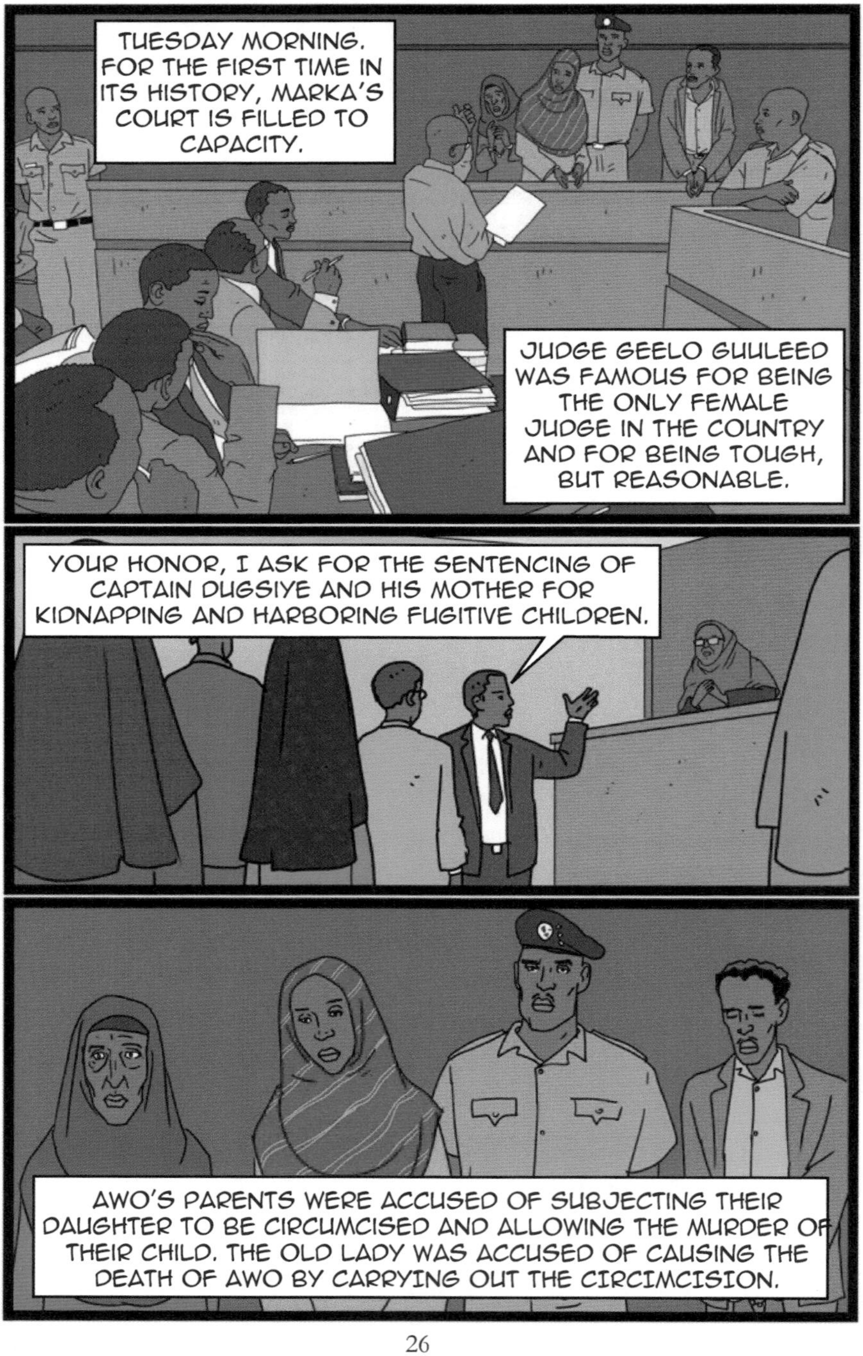
TUESDAY MORNING. FOR THE FIRST TIME IN ITS HISTORY, MARKA'S COURT IS FILLED TO CAPACITY.
JUDGE GEELO GUULEED WAS FAMOUS FOR BEING THE ONLY FEMALE JUDGE IN THE COUNTRY AND FOR BEING TOUGH, BUT REASONABLE.
YOUR HONOR, I ASK FOR THE SENTENCING OF CAPTAIN DUGSIYE AND HIS MOTHER FOR KIDNAPPING AND HARBORING FUGITIVE CHILDREN.
AWO'S PARENTS WERE ACCUSED OF SUBJECTING THEIR DAUGHTER TO BE CIRCUMCISED AND ALLOWING THE MURDER OF THEIR CHILD. THE OLD LADY WAS ACCUSED OF CAUSING THE DEATH OF AWO BY CARRYING OUT THE CIRCIMCISION.

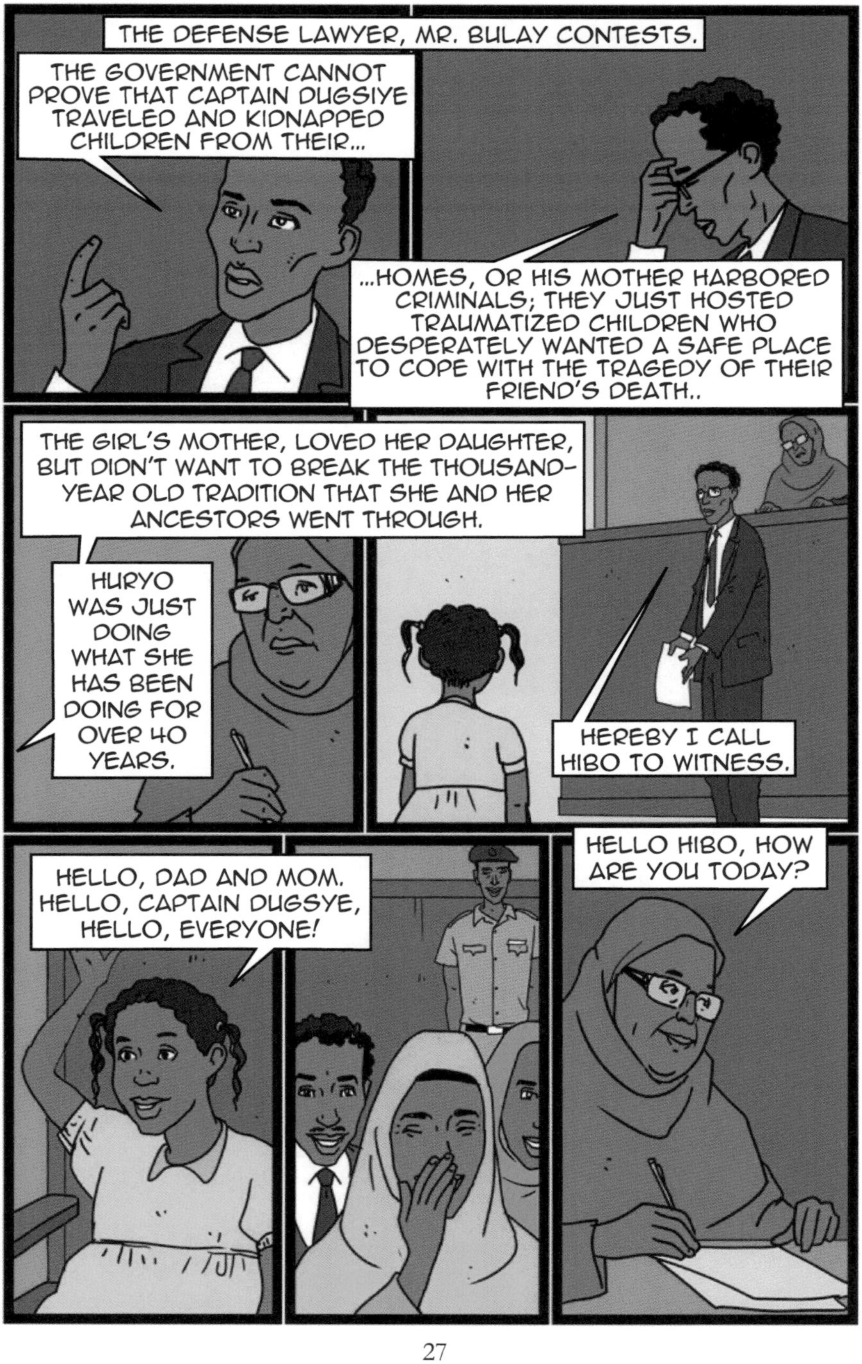
THE DEFENSE LAWYER, MR. BULAY CONTESTS.
THE GOVERNMENT CANNOT PROVE THAT CAPTAIN DUGSIYE TRAVELED AND KIDNAPPED CHILDREN FROM THEIR...
...HOMES, OR HIS MOTHER HARBORED CRIMINALS; THEY JUST HOSTED TRAUMATIZED CHILDREN WHO DESPERATELY WANTED A SAFE PLACE TO COPE WITH THE TRAGEDY OF THEIR FRIEND'S DEATH..
THE GIRL'S MOTHER, LOVED HER DAUGHTER, BUT DIDN'T WANT TO BREAK THE THOUSAND-YEAR OLD TRADITION THAT SHE AND HER ANCESTORS WENT THROUGH.
HURYO WAS JUST DOING WHAT SHE HAS BEEN DOING FOR OVER 40 YEARS.
HEREBY I CALL HIBO TO WITNESS.
HELLO, DAD AND MOM. HELLO, CAPTAIN DUGSYE, HELLO, EVERYONE!
HELLO HIBO, HOW ARE YOU TODAY?

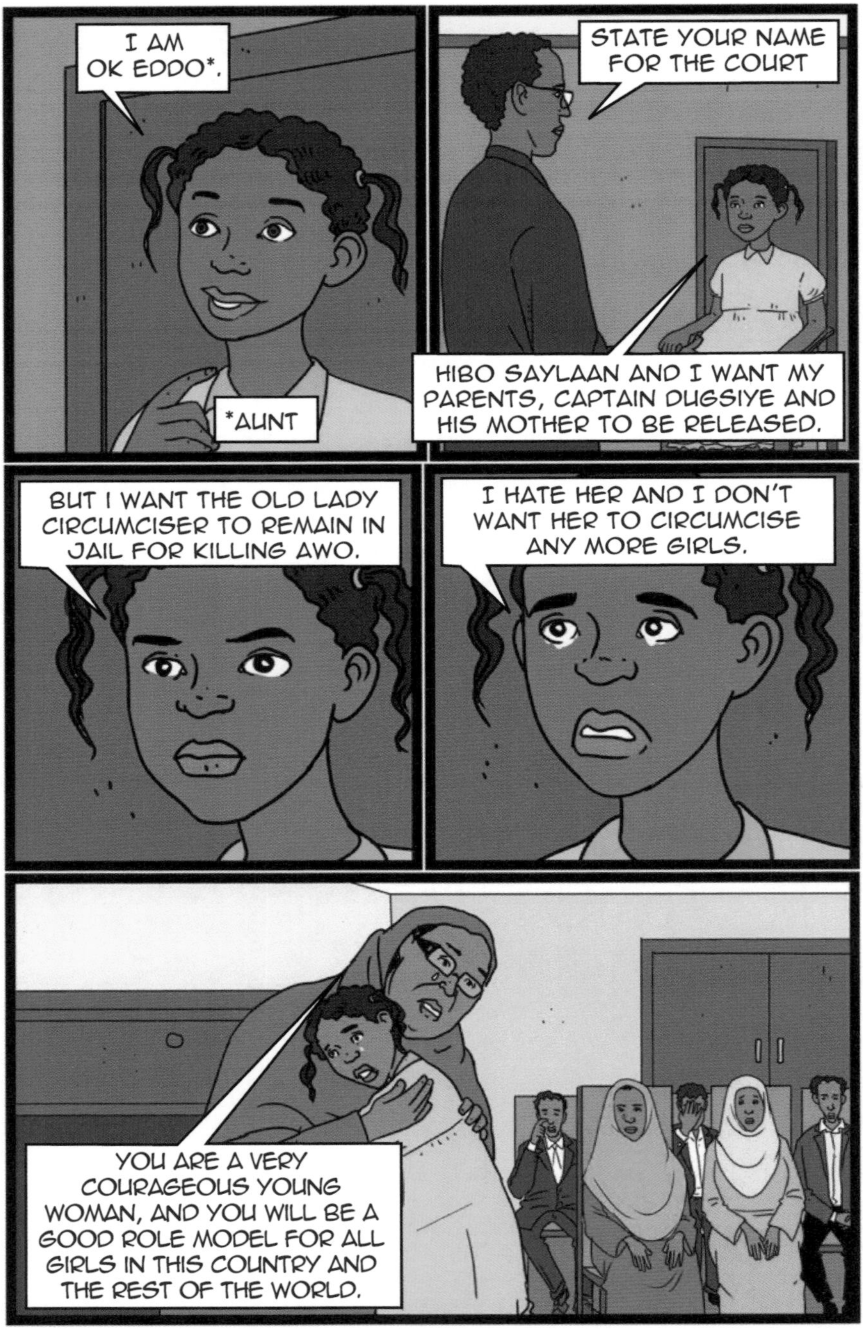
I AM OK EDDO*.
*AUNT
STATE YOUR NAME FOR THE COURT
HIBO SAYLAAN AND I WANT MY PARENTS, CAPTAIN DUGSIYE AND HIS MOTHER TO BE RELEASED.
BUT I WANT THE OLD LADY CIRCUMCISER TO REMAIN IN JAIL FOR KILLING AWO.
I HATE HER AND I DON'T WANT HER TO CIRCUMCISE ANY MORE GIRLS.
YOU ARE A VERY COURAGEOUS YOUNG WOMAN, AND YOU WILL BE A GOOD ROLE MODEL FOR ALL GIRLS IN THIS COUNTRY AND THE REST OF THE WORLD.

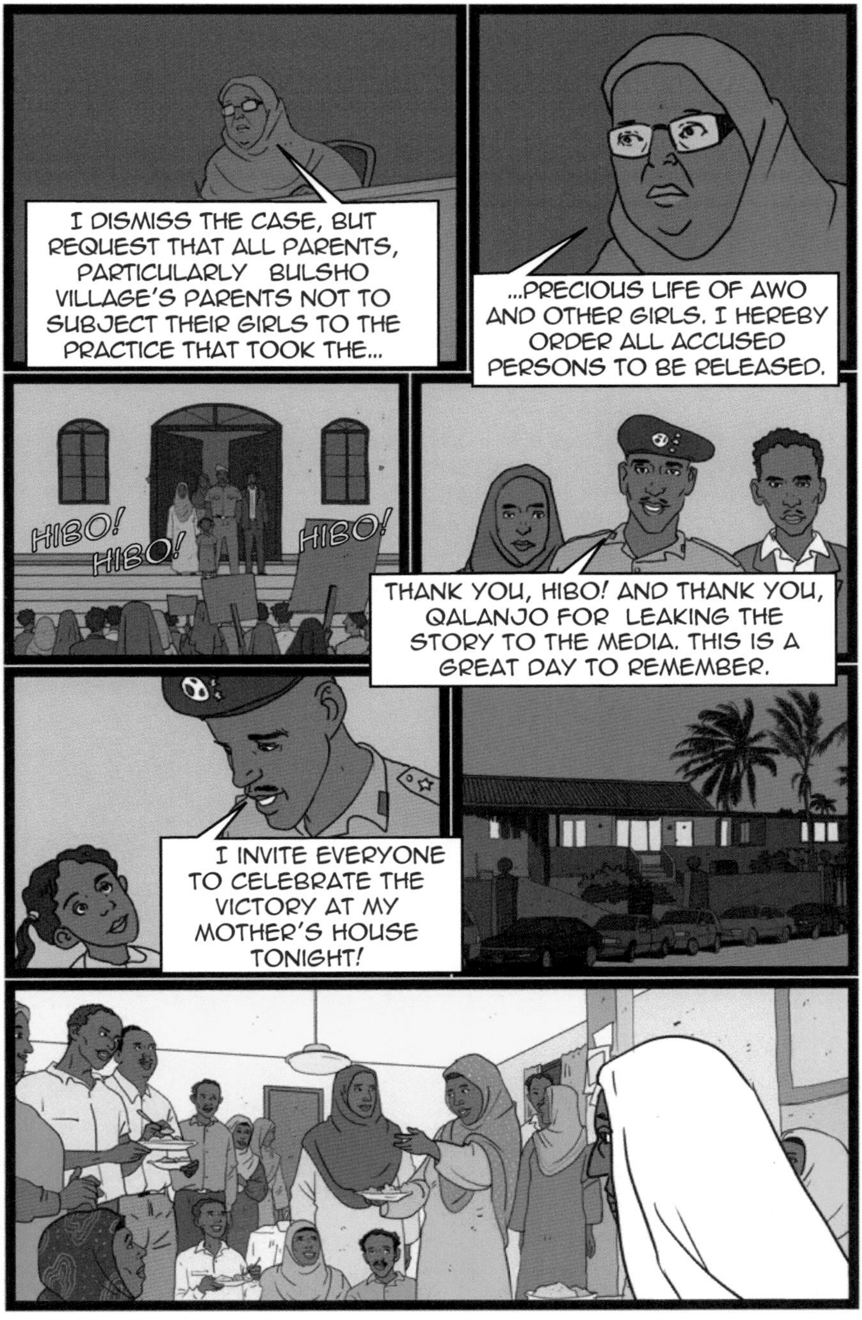
I DISMISS THE CASE, BUT REQUEST THAT ALL PARENTS, PARTICULARLY BULSHO VILLAGE'S PARENTS NOT TO SUBJECT THEIR GIRLS TO THE PRACTICE THAT TOOK THE...
...PRECIOUS LIFE OF AWO AND OTHER GIRLS. I HEREBY ORDER ALL ACCUSED PERSONS TO BE RELEASED.
HIBO! HIBO! HIBO!
THANK YOU, HIBO! AND THANK YOU, QALANJO FOR LEAKING THE STORY TO THE MEDIA. THIS IS A GREAT DAY TO REMEMBER.
I INVITE EVERYONE TO CELEBRATE THE VICTORY AT MY MOTHER'S HOUSE TONIGHT!

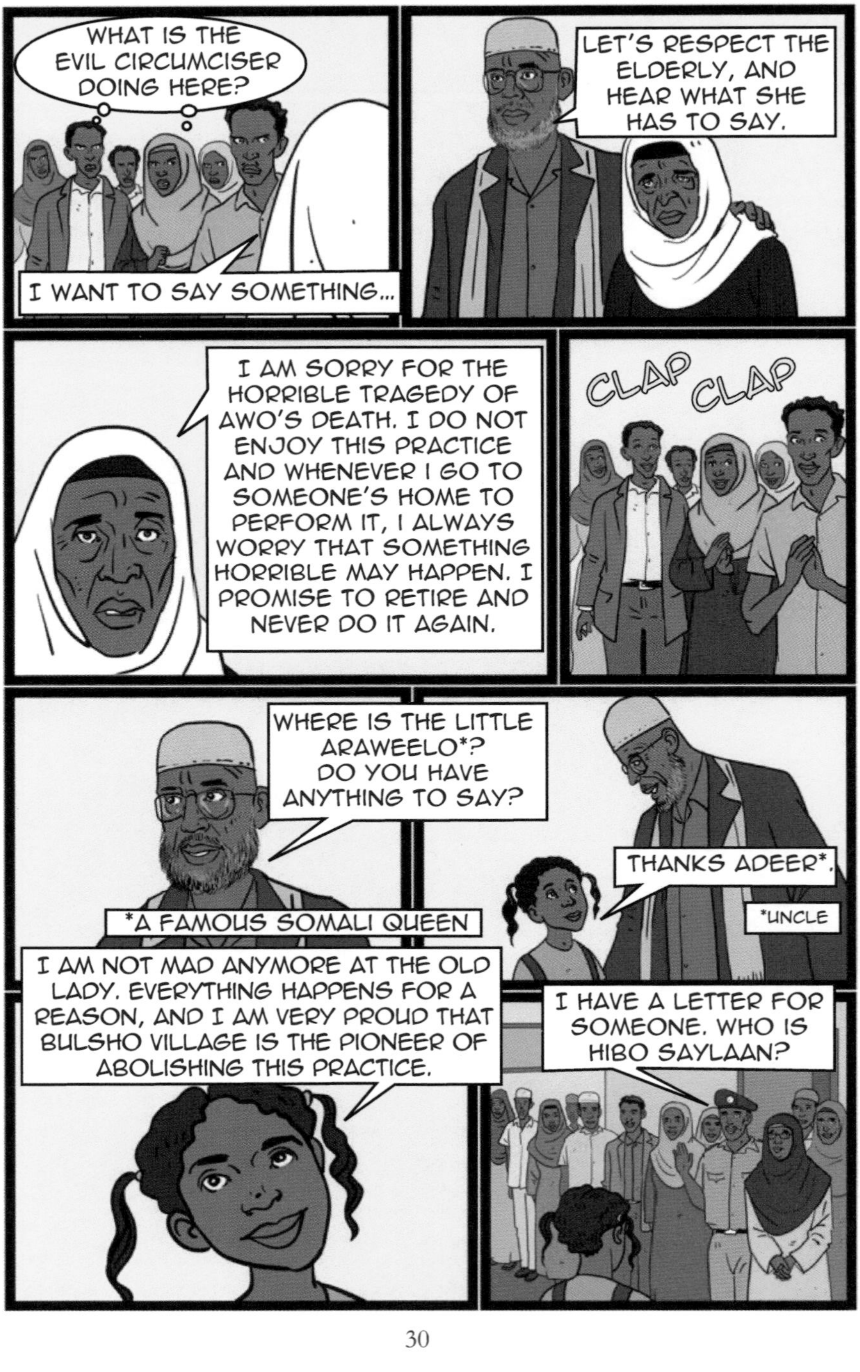
WHAT IS THE EVIL CIRCUMCISER DOING HERE?
I WANT TO SAY SOMETHING...
LET'S RESPECT THE ELDERLY, AND HEAR WHAT SHE HAS TO SAY.
I AM SORRY FOR THE HORRIBLE TRAGEDY OF AWO'S DEATH. I DO NOT ENJOY THIS PRACTICE AND WHENEVER I GO TO SOMEONE'S HOME TO PERFORM IT, I ALWAYS WORRY THAT SOMETHING HORRIBLE MAY HAPPEN. I PROMISE TO RETIRE AND NEVER DO IT AGAIN.
CLAP CLAP
WHERE IS THE LITTLE ARAWEELO*? DO YOU HAVE ANYTHING TO SAY?
*A FAMOUS SOMALI QUEEN
THANKS ADEER*.
*UNCLE
I AM NOT MAD ANYMORE AT THE OLD LADY. EVERYTHING HAPPENS FOR A REASON, AND I AM VERY PROUD THAT BULSHO VILLAGE IS THE PIONEER OF ABOLISHING THIS PRACTICE.
I HAVE A LETTER FOR SOMEONE. WHO IS HIBO SAYLAAN?

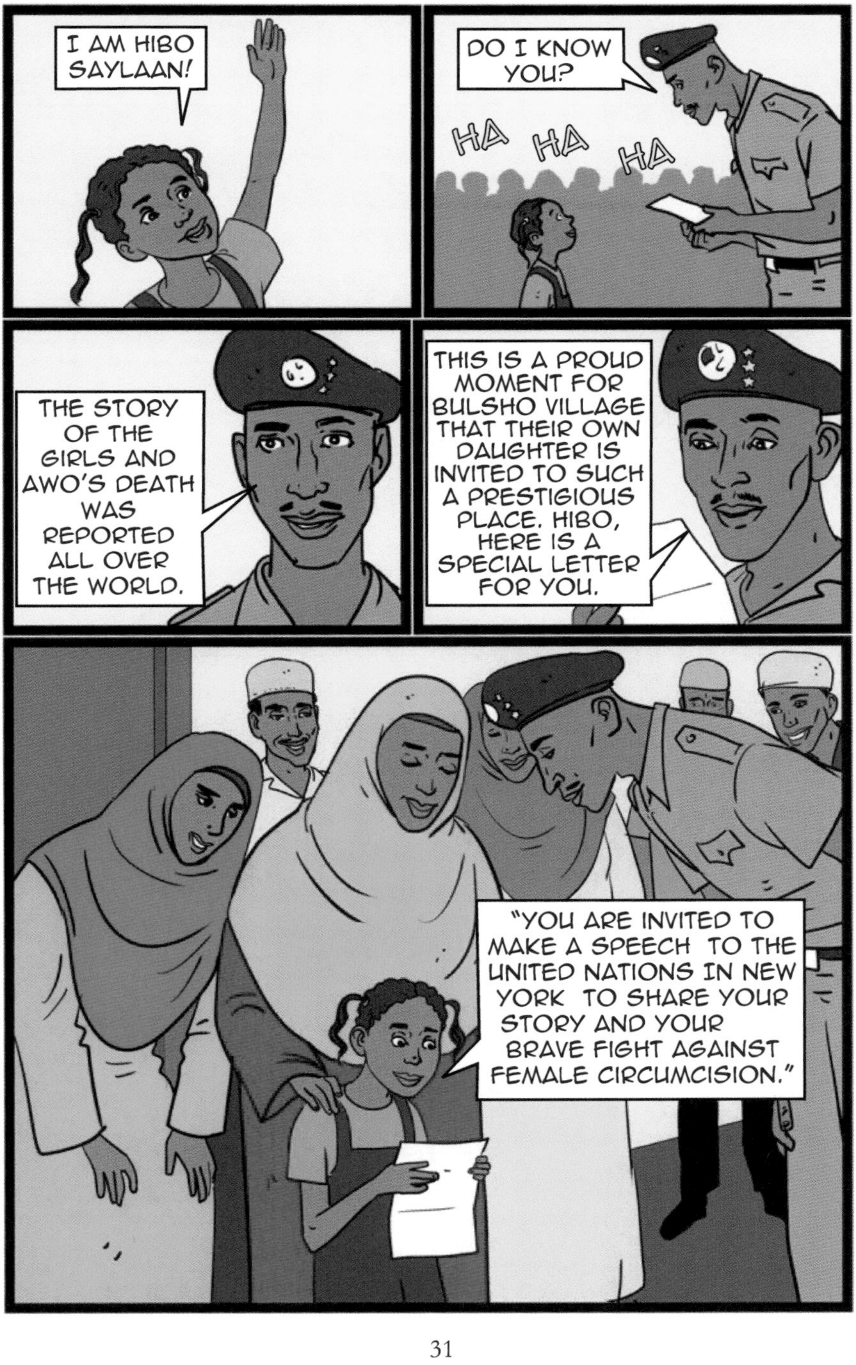

I AM HIBO SAYLAAN!
DO I KNOW YOU?
HA HA HA
THE STORY OF THE GIRLS AND AWO'S DEATH WAS REPORTED ALL OVER THE WORLD.
THIS IS A PROUD MOMENT FOR BULSHO VILLAGE THAT THEIR OWN DAUGHTER IS INVITED TO SUCH A PRESTIGIOUS PLACE. HIBO, HERE IS A SPECIAL LETTER FOR YOU.
"YOU ARE INVITED TO MAKE A SPEECH TO THE UNITED NATIONS IN NEW YORK TO SHARE YOUR STORY AND YOUR BRAVE FIGHT AGAINST FEMALE CIRCUMCISION."

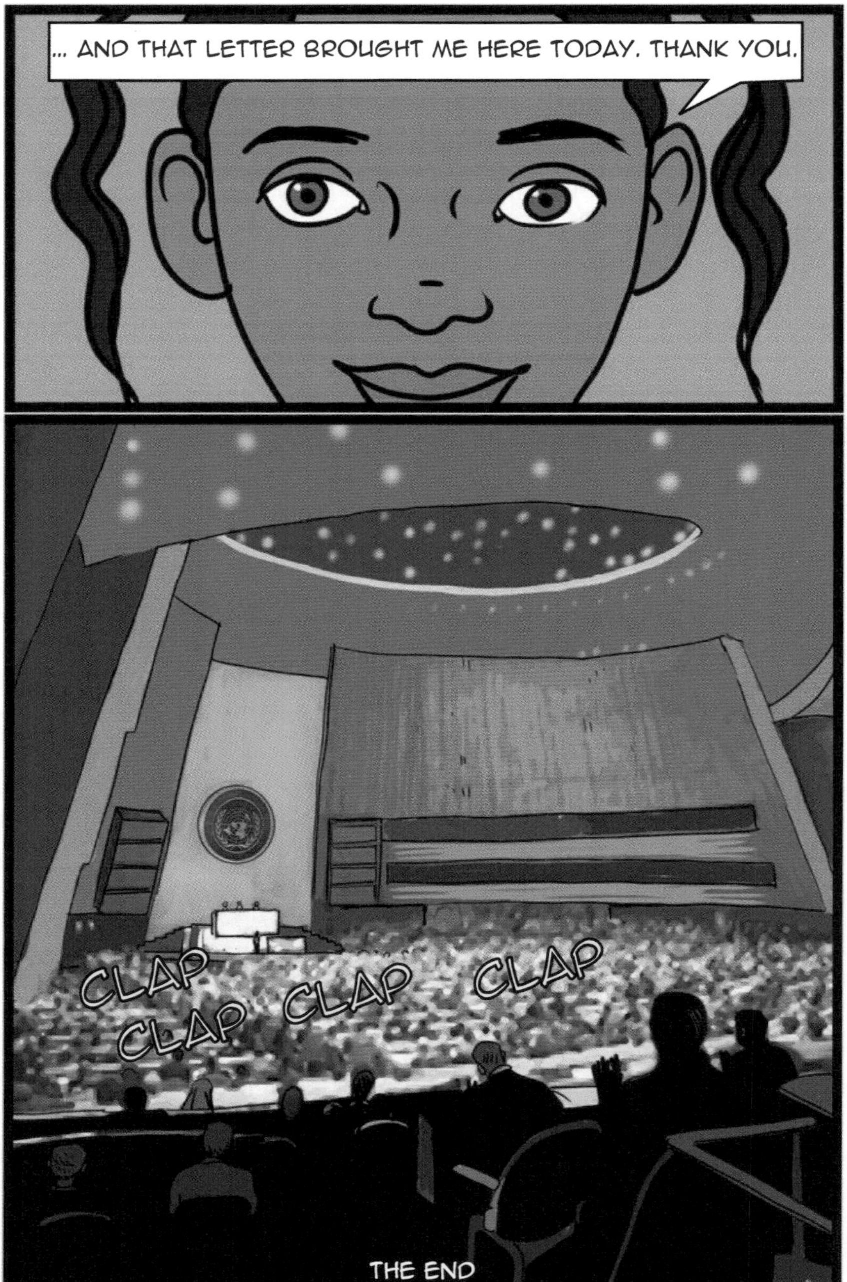
... AND THAT LETTER BROUGHT ME HERE TODAY. THANK YOU.
CLAP
CLAP
CLAP
CLAP
THE END

39534339R00024

Made in the USA
Charleston, SC
12 March 2015